Stephen Fredman asserts in his latest work that American poetry is groundless – that each generation of American poets faces the problem of identity anew and has to discover fresh meaning for itself. His argument focuses on four pairs of poets – Eliot/Williams, Thoreau/Olson, Emerson/Duncan, and Whitman/Creeley – and points out that although the later ones all were influenced by their predecessors to some extent, ultimately their poetry is, paradoxically, grounded in an essential groundlessness.

In order to demonstrate how approaches to groundlessness have persisted over time, Fredman explores the various measures taken by these American poets to provide a provisional ground upon which to construct their poetry: inventing idiosyncratic traditions, forming poetic communities, engaging in polemical prose, assessing all the dimensions of particular places, and treating words as emblematic and mysterious objects. At the very core of the book stands Charles Olson, whose work so dramatically articulates the whole range of issues arising from the American poet's anxious search for, and resistance to, an authentic and unified tradition.

CAMBRIDGE STUDIES IN AMERICAN LITERATURE AND CULTURE

The grounding of American poetry

Continued on pages following the Index

The grounding of
American poetry

Charles Olson and the Emersonian tradition

STEPHEN FREDMAN

Department of English
University of Notre Dame

CAMBRIDGE
UNIVERSITY PRESS

Published by the Press Syndicate of the University of Cambridge
The Pitt Building, Trumpington Street, Cambridge CB2 1RP
40 West 20th Street, New York, NY 10011-4211, USA
10 Stamford Road, Oakleigh, Victoria 3166, Australia

© Cambridge University Press 1993

First published 1993

Printed in the United States of America

Library of Congress Cataloging-in-Publication Data
Fredman, Stephen, 1948–

The grounding of American poetry : Charles Olson and the Emersonian tradition /
Stephen Fredman.

p.   cm. – (Cambridge studies in American literature and culture; 67)

Includes index

ISBN 0-521-44303-2

1. Olson, Charles, 1910–1970 – Criticism and interpretation.   2. American poetry –
History and criticism – Theory, etc.   3. Emerson, Ralph Waldo, 1803–1882 – Influence.
4. Influence (Literary, artistic, etc.)   I. Title.   II. Series.
PS3529.L655Z65   1993
811'.009 – dc20   92-40123
                                                                                                              CIP

A catalog record for this book is available from the British Library.

ISBN 0-521-44303-2 hardback

The following works are reprinted by permission of New Directions Publishing Corporation: "The Resistance," Charles Olson, from *Selected Writings,* copyright © 1966 by Charles Olson; "This World," Robert Creeley, from *Later,* copyright © 1979 by Robert Creeley; "Such Is the Sickness of Many a Good Thing," "Moira's Cathedral," "Transgressing the Real," Robert Duncan, from *Bending the Bow,* copyright © 1968 by Robert Duncan; "The Dance," Robert Duncan, from *The Opening of the Field,* copyright © 1960 by Robert Duncan. Quotations from Charles Olson, *The Maximus Poems,* edited by George F. Butterick, copyright © 1983 by The Regents of the University of California, are reprinted by permission of the University of California Press.

CONTENTS

PREFACE

In this book I would like to explore an underlying condition of American poetry that helps to account for much of what I find most distinctive, provocative, and problematic about it. The condition can be described simply: since it has been a "modern" undertaking from the outset, American poetry lacks grounding in a unified tradition. From its inception in the Renaissance and the Reformation, the modern, by definition, has been that which breaks with tradition. America has always been situated in this rupture. As Roy Harvey Pearce said over thirty years ago, "The 'Americanness' of American poetry is, quite simply, its compulsive 'modernism.'" Finding themselves in this rupture, American poets, especially since Emerson, have responded to the modern condition by engaging in two inextricably intertwined enterprises, which I would like to designate as modernism and grounding. Modernism, as an esthetic movement, confronts the rupture of the modern by embracing its unsettling quality through formal innovation. The inventions of modernism work to destroy traditional contexts and to create new unities through purely formal means, such as the collage. Grounding, on the other hand, seeks to reinvent context, to dig down into the site of rupture in the hope of finding, not the old tradition or a new tradition, but the basis of tradition. Lacking the authority a long-standing tradition confers, American poets have had to invent alternative, provisional ways of grounding their poetry, thus assuming the work of tradition in the absence of a unified context.

The enterprises of modernism and grounding run together throughout American poetry and through particular American poets. In an earlier book, *Poet's Prose: The Crisis in American Verse,* I dealt with modernism in poetry at one of its extreme edges, the boundary between poetry and prose. This book looks primarily at grounding, which is the less apparent, though possibly more pervasive, of the two American responses to the rupture of the modern. In keeping with this perspective,

modernist poets of the twentieth century, in whom the emphasis upon
modernism is particularly strong, take a back seat here – as do their most
profound inheritors among contemporary poets, the Language poets. At
the forefront are the projectivist poets, especially Charles Olson, Robert
Duncan, and Robert Creeley, and right behind them stand the transcendentalists, especially Thoreau, Emerson, and Whitman; the similar methods of grounding employed by these two groups of poets make for a
fruitful comparative study. By engaging in the modernist gesture of
separating the projectivists and the transcendentalists from the whole of
the fledgling tradition of Emersonian poetry in America, I hope to bring
the enterprise of grounding into the light as a major characteristic of
American poetry.

Charles Olson was chosen as the central focus of this study because his
work so dramatically articulates the whole range of issues that arise from
the American preoccupation with grounding. Rather than present an
exhaustive study of American poetry, I have clustered a series of rela-
tionships and issues around Olson in concentric circles of increasing
suggestiveness. The following diagram gives a schematic approximation
of the organization.

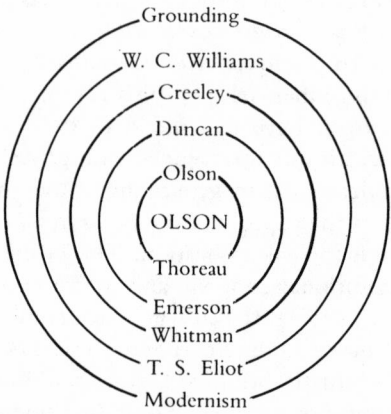

In keeping with this manner of presentation, there are three chapters on
Olson, in which Henry David Thoreau's *Walden* serves as a background
text, and which take up half of the book; a quarter of the study is devoted
to a long chapter on Robert Duncan and Ralph Waldo Emerson; the
conclusion focuses on Robert Creeley, using Walt Whitman's "Out of the
Cradle Endlessly Rocking" as background; and the first chapter looks at
the relationship between modernism and grounding in William Carlos
Williams's *In the American Grain* and T. S. Eliot's "Tradition and the
Individual Talent."

This undertaking began in 1982 with the intuition that the projectivists and the transcendentalists share something in common, and that if I could understand what this something is I might have a way of accounting for basic qualities of American poetry that I had never seen satisfactorily explained. During that year, I was able to begin the research and the thinking for this project, thanks to fellowships from the National Endowment for the Humanities and the American Council of Learned Societies, and with space provided generously by the Newberry Library in Chicago. Because what I am speaking about in this study is both subtle and widely pervasive, it has not been easy to conceptualize. There have been several false starts. One, for instance, was the notion that groups of poets operate like baseball teams – that while constituting themselves as a team by their shared opposition to prevailing orthodoxies, the different poets on the team would play different positions. This seemed like a way to account both for the sense of belonging that groups of American poets have cultivated and for the wide diversities of styles, beliefs, and values among the individual poets within these groups. Over time, the team metaphor came to seem too restricted – although I hope that I have kept the valid insights it contained – and I was forced to pursue new metaphors and concepts.

This process of creation and destruction took place several times before the summer of 1988, when I realized that, instead of trying so hard to translate the ideas and images I was developing into chapters about particular American poets, I would do better just to sit down and write whatever I had to say about one poet, Charles Olson. Almost immediately, I saw that Olson and Thoreau share a method of grounding their writing, which I have called "containment." Out of this insight, the book as a whole took shape. During that summer I wrote fast, and I had the pleasure of discussing the work, section by section, with the poet and critic John Matthias, whose profound understanding of Olson made him an ideal sounding board.

This study has benefited from the aid not only of the institutions mentioned above but also from grants by the Institute for Study of the Liberal Arts at the University of Notre Dame and from interactions with a large number of individuals. At various times, most of my colleagues in the Notre Dame Department of English and students in my graduate and undergraduate courses have listened to the ideas and enthusiasms that were gestating toward this work, and their responses have enhanced it. *Twentieth Century Literature* and *North Dakota Quarterly* provided forums for earlier versions of Chapters 1 and 6, for which I am grateful.

Finally, I would like to thank a few individuals, both at Notre Dame and elsewhere, for their decisive contributions to this book: Gerald

Bruns, Joseph Buttigieg, Albert Gelpi, Theresa Krier, Greg Kucich, John Matthias, Sherman Paul, Marjorie Perloff, Linda Taylor, and Thomas Werge. I hope that the love and support provided during this time by Katherine and Nicholas Fredman and by Swami Chidvilasananda shine through it all.

LIST OF ABBREVIATIONS

The following abbreviations for works frequently cited are used in the notes and short-form notations in the text.

AP Charles Olson, *Additional Prose,* ed. George F. Butterick. Bolinas, Calif.: Four Seasons Foundation, 1974.

BB Robert Duncan, *Bending the Bow.* New York: New Directions, 1968.

Boer Charles Boer, *Charles Olson in Connecticut.* Chicago: Swallow Press, 1975.

Clark Tom Clark, *Charles Olson: The Allegory of a Poet's Life.* New York: W. W. Norton, 1991.

CP *The Collected Poems of Charles Olson,* ed. George F. Butterick. Berkeley: Univ. of California Press, 1987.

FC Robert Duncan, *Fictive Certainties.* New York: New Directions, 1985.

GW Robert Duncan, *Ground Work: Before the War.* New York: New Directions, 1984.

HD 1.3 Robert Duncan, *H. D. Book,* "Part I, Chapter 3," *Tri-Quarterly,* 12 (Spring 1968):67–82.

HD 1.5 Robert Duncan, *H. D. Book,* "Part I, Chapter 5," *Stony Brook,* 1/2 (Fall 1968):4–19.

HU Charles Olson, *Human Universe and Other Essays,* ed. Donald Allen. New York: Grove Press, 1967.

IAG William Carlos Williams, *In the American Grain.* 1925; rpt. New York: New Directions, 1956.

LG   Walt Whitman, *Leaves of Grass,* ed. Sculley Bradley and Harold W. Blodgett. New York: Norton, 1973.

Max   Charles Olson, *The Maximus Poems,* ed. George F. Butterick. Berkeley: Univ. of California Press, 1983.

Muth I   Charles Olson, *Muthologos: The Collected Lectures & Interviews,* vol. 1, ed. George F. Butterick. Bolinas, Calif.: Four Seasons Foundation, 1978.

Muth II   Charles Olson, *Muthologos: The Collected Lectures & Interviews,* vol. 2, ed. George F. Butterick. Bolinas, Calif.: Four Seasons Foundation, 1979.

OF   Robert Duncan, *The Opening of the Field.* New York: Grove Press, 1960.

QG   Robert Creeley, *A Quick Graph: Collected Notes & Essays,* ed. Donald Allen. San Francisco: Four Seasons Foundation, 1970.

RWE   *Selected Writings of Ralph Waldo Emerson,* ed. William H. Gilman. New York: New American Library, 1965.

Senses   Stanley Cavell, *The Senses of Walden,* expanded ed. San Francisco: North Point, 1981.

SP   *The Selected Prose of T. S. Eliot,* ed. Frank Kermode. New York: Harcourt Brace Jovanovich, 1975.

SVH   Charles Olson, *The Special View of History,* ed. Ann Charters. Berkeley: Oyez, 1970.

SW   Charles Olson, *Selected Writings,* ed. Robert Creeley. New York: New Directions, 1966.

T   Edward Shils, *Tradition.* Chicago: Univ. of Chicago Press, 1981.

T&M   Hans-Georg Gadamer, *Truth and Method.* 2d rev. ed. Trans. W. Glen-Doepel; trans. rev. by Joel Weinsheimer and Donald Marshall. New York: Crossroad, 1992.

W   Henry David Thoreau, *Walden and Civil Disobedience,* ed. Owen Thomas. New York: Norton, 1966.

INTRODUCTION

In 1950 a young German poet, Rainer Maria Gerhardt, established contact with the American poets Robert Creeley and Charles Olson. Gerhardt was beginning an international little magazine, in German, *Fragmente* (whose title alludes to the "fragments" of T. S. Eliot's *Waste Land*), for which he hoped to solicit new American poetry in the Poundian tradition. As the correspondence progressed and Gerhardt read works by Creeley and Olson, he developed a sense of kinship with the two emerging American poets, and in December of 1950 he wrote "Letter to Creeley and Olson," an epistolary poem in six "montages."[1]

Although in his "Letter" Gerhardt adopted the visual form of Olson's poetry, he relied especially heavily upon Pound, whom he had translated, by alluding to images from the "Pisan Cantos," by updating "Hugh Selwyn Mauberly" to the post–World War II era, and by splicing together fragments of world civilization:

>   one ought to
>   the passport to America   going home
>   via the Punjab and Indus valley in the tracks
>   of poets
>   of language
>   through jungle and waste
>   passing the islands
>   of huge dogheaded
>   birds
>   meals of white mash and pap
>   sprinkled with ashes
>   the sails
>   Francesca's
>   but Dante will not let us live
>   always the fields to be harvested

1

> always the same sky above the bent-over backs
> earth-burdened
> and in rain the house
> the long departed souls[2]

Gerhardt had a strong desire to join in the new projectivist movement that Olson and Creeley were inaugurating in America, but he felt trapped by the burden of the European past, by the need to follow "in the tracks / of poets." The young German poet experienced history as suffocating and incapacitating: "the long departed souls" are everywhere and "Dante will not let us live." He expressed the wish for a "passport to America," to a place of literary experimentation beyond the confines of tradition.

Olson wrote a poem in reply, "To Gerhardt, There, Among Europe's Things of Which He Has Written Us in His 'Brief an Creeley und Olson,' " in which he issued an invitation: "If you want to shut yourself in, shut yourself in / If you do not want to shut yourself in, come out" (*CP*, 212). Olson offered Gerhardt two ways to come out: he could delve beneath European tradition until he reached the paleolithic (from which Olson presented him with a myth about Old Man Bear); or he could

> . . . come here
> where we will welcome you
> with nothing but what is, with
> no useful allusions, with no birds
> but those we stone, nothing to eat
> but ourselves, no end and no beginning, I assure you, yet
> not at all primitive, living as we do in a space we do not need to
> contrive   (*CP*, 219)

As an "archaeologist of morning," Olson believed that it was possible to dig through to firm ground, in a self-sustaining relationship to both nature and culture, wherever one stood, in Europe or in America, and he invited Gerhardt to ground himself in either locale. Olson summed up his advice to Gerhardt in a later essay: "go out the back door of your inheritance" (*HU*, 155).

But, as Creeley said of the brave though melancholy Gerhardt, "There was no way to move in any easy sense beyond the past, and there never will be" (*QG*, 223). For Gerhardt, as a European poet, the burden of tradition may have been absolutely inescapable. But what about the American poet? Does the American poet, too, inherit a brilliant but suffocating tradition? Speaking of the narrowness and lack of encouragement he encountered when young, Creeley testifies:

To begin with, I was shy of the word "poet" and all its associations in a world I was then intimate with. It was not, in short, a fit attention for a young man raised in the New England manner, compact of Puritanically deprived senses of speech and sensuality. Life was real and life was earnest, and one had best get on with it. (QG, 61)

For the young Creeley, European tradition was not smothering, for the simple reason that it was never fully present as a commanding repository of values. In America, the attitude that life is real and life is earnest, and one had best get on with it, is not reserved only for philistines. American poets, too, share in the general American sense "that they, perhaps more than any other group of people upon the earth at this moment, have had to both imagine and thereby to *make* that reality which they are then given to live in. It is as though they had to *realize* the world anew" (QG, 65). Americans have the frightening and exhilarating experience of standing on shaky ground; they work, as Gerhardt notes, "in the new shaft the bulwarks lacking" (192). Having plunged ahead to forge the "new shaft," they have often wondered where the "bulwarks" are.

Recognizing this dilemma, American poets have sought a number of ways to "*realize* the world anew"; unavoidably, this task has become a central preoccupation of American poetry. In this book, I will investigate some of the ways in which the issue of grounding has been framed and addressed within the Emersonian lineage of American poetry. As in a previous book, *Poet's Prose,* my method will involve primarily an investigation of prose by American poets.[3] Here I will not focus upon the prose written as poetry but rather upon the prose written as "bulwark" for the poetry. That is, in the absence of an embracing cultural tradition, the prose statements perform an important duty by authorizing the poetry. An awareness of this crucial quality of the prose is absolutely essential for reading American poetry. There is a theatrical quality to the prose that creates a mise-en-scène for the poetry, a context in which the poem can be performed. When readers isolate a particular American poem and debate whether it "works," they often miss the "work" of American poetry. Reading a poem by Charles Olson for the first time, for example, many readers complain about stylistic infelicities, such as ungainliness or corniness, and wonder how this apparently awkward poet merits such high regard among his partisans. A significant portion of the answer lies in Olson's prose essays, which prepare his readers not by engaging in some sort of special pleading for his poetry but by creating such a powerful staging for it that his poetry gains a context in which it can become affecting and convincing work. Lacking a grounded tradition to draw upon, Olson uses his essays, lectures, interviews, book reviews, and letters to present an alternative grounding method I call "containment," which makes his poetry both possible and effective.

In this book, I want to investigate the necessarily provisional and ultimately paradoxical grounding methods employed by a range of American poets, in order to show how essential these methods are to American poetry and how pervasive their effects upon that poetry are. Most often, poets from the transcendentalists and the projectivist movements will be juxtaposed, in the interests of pointing out long-range continuities of method without belaboring specific issues of influence. For example, in the case of Robert Duncan, Ezra Pound is probably his most formative influence, and Duncan has also written at great length about Walt Whitman and even incorporated the nineteenth-century poet into his own poems; rather than explore these lines of influence, however, I will place Duncan's work against the background of Ralph Waldo Emerson's essays, to highlight a basic similarity in approach to the issue of grounding. In the course of the study the following pairs are treated: Eliot and Williams, Olson and Thoreau, Duncan and Emerson, and Creeley and Whitman. After a first chapter on the question of tradition, using as examples the modernists Williams and Eliot, the study focuses upon projectivist poets as primary figures and transcendentalists as background figures. The first chapter, "Williams, Eliot, and American Tradition," sets forth in some detail the issue of tradition and the American poetic responses to it, pointing to Eliot and Williams, who appear to be opposites in so many ways, as brother creators of "separate but equal" idiosyncratic traditions in their prose works, "Tradition and the Individual Talent" and *In the American Grain*. The next three chapters investigate the method of containment in Olson's prose and his *Maximus Poems* and in Thoreau's *Walden*. The first of these chapters, "Finding Out for Oneself," explores containment as a spiritual discipline; the second chapter considers the politics of "Resistance and Poetic Community"; and the third, "The Poetics of Recognition," discusses the esthetic ramifications of containment. The grounding method identified in the fifth chapter, "Circles and Boundaries," applies to Duncan and Emerson, for whom circling both provides bounded wholes and encourages disruptive transgressions. The material for this chapter derives primarily from Emerson's essay "Circles" and from Duncan's poetry and the prose of *Fictive Certainties*. The first part of the Conclusion focuses upon the method of repetition in the poetry of Whitman's "Out of the Cradle Endlessly Rocking" and Creeley's "This World." The second part of the chapter uses an essay by Creeley, "I'm given to write poems," to draw forth and summarize five modes of alternative grounding that are found consistently within and often beyond the Emersonian lineage: the idiosyncratic tradition, the poetic community, the hieroglyphic or "picture-writing" mode, the inscription of place, and the uses of prose.

The more particular methods of containment, circling, and repetition comprise the characteristic ways by which the respective pairs of projectivist and transcendentalist poets approach the condition of groundlessness. While engaged in a single method, each of these poets employs a variety of alternative grounding modes. It is important to stress from the outset, however, that such modes are always provisional and that the most profound aspect of poetic methods like containment, circling, and repetition is their ability to honor and even make use of groundlessness while simultaneously compensating for it. This is the most telling fact about American poetry. In discussing Emerson, for instance, Stanley Cavell pictures this kind of mobile grounding in the face of groundlessness as a salutary "abandonment." This abandonment entails, he claims, the qualities of enthusiasm, freedom from the past, and trusting oneself to the road, and Americans perpetually reenact this abandonment as they attempt to counter the despair that can arise when one feels unable to begin an enterprise for lack of authorization:

> [Emerson's] perception of the moment is taken in hope, as something to be proven only on the way, *by* the way. This departure, such setting out, is, in our poverty, what hope consists in, all there is to hope for, it is the abandoning of despair, which is otherwise our condition. (Quiet desperation Thoreau will call it; Emerson had said, silent melancholy.) Hence he may speak of perception as "not Whimsical, but fatal." . . . We hope it is better than whim at last, as we hope we may at least seem something better than blasphemers; but it is our poverty not to be final but always to be leaving (abandoning whatever we have and have known): to be initial, medial, American.[4]

Americans wish to be "initial" or "medial" but not "final." In that sense, we could think of all the poetry in the Emersonian tradition as hopeful "essays." As Cavell indicates, there is a healthy dose of abandon built into the grounding projects of American poets. The construction of an idiosyncratic tradition or the creation of a poetic community, for instance, represents the hope of finding a place to stand while on the open road.

Chapter 1

WILLIAMS, ELIOT, AND AMERICAN TRADITION

"TRADITION . . . CANNOT BE INHERITED"

What do American poets do to get situated as poets? How do they find their bearings? This has always been a different question for American poets than it has been for poets in societies for which tradition more fully lays out the ground (for example, Europe, the Islamic world, India, China, Japan, and various tribal societies). The relationship of America to European tradition is, as the novels of Henry James depict in consummate fashion, a highly complex one: we are neither definitively separate from nor wholly subsumed within European tradition, neither outsiders nor insiders. William Carlos Williams puts it in terms very similar to those used by his disciple Creeley: "To Americans the effort to appraise the real through the maze of a cut-off and imposed culture from Europe has been a vivid task, if very often too great for their realizations."[1] In America there is much for a poet to discover – for instance, where to stand in relation to the rest of the populace, whether there has yet been a successful American poetry or whether it must still be invented, and if there is any value in writing poetry at all. And does it make sense to think of poetry in the traditional way as a "calling" or an "office" when we seem to have no way of recognizing whence or in whose name a call is issued or an office assigned?

Foundational questions confront an American poet: Where is the ground of American poetry? How does an American poet feel authorized to speak? Because of the insistence of these questions, the existential issue of finding one's bearings, which in more traditional societies marks the onset of a life in poetry, remains critical throughout many an American poet's career. Our poets characteristically address the lack of authority by inventing ways to claim a ground while simultaneously insuring that the ground not be "fixed." Unwilling or unable to inherit a tradition that presents itself as a stable ground, our poets invent provisional ground-

6

ings, while at the same time restlessly overstepping the limits of any constituted ground. This paradoxical endeavor of situating a poetry while allowing the ground to fluctuate makes the best of the unprecedented challenges and opportunities of American culture, giving our poetry a salutary philosophical and spiritual adventurousness.

Regarded for so long as polar opposites within the geography of modernism, both William Carlos Williams and T. S. Eliot engage in appropriations of tradition that demonstrate one of the desperate but productive ways in which American poets situate themselves. Although Eliot's "Tradition and the Individual Talent" is usually seen as a wholehearted return to European tradition and Williams's *In the American Grain* is customarily taken as a celebration of "true" nativism, both of these readings disregard the crucial issue of grounding, in light of which they metamorphose into a supplementary pair. Both poets construct idiosyncratic traditions out of historical materials, looking for a cultural frame in which to locate their own texts. After modernism, poets like Charles Olson and Robert Duncan take a slightly different stance toward an authorizing tradition – allowing the frame to dissolve by opening the poetry to encounters with an otherness that is beyond the poet's control.

The sociologist Edward Shils offers a succinct discussion of the centrality of tradition to social life in his book *Tradition,* which had its inception, coincidentally, as the T. S. Eliot Memorial Lectures at the University of Kent. In the preface, Shils declares himself an inheritor of Eliot, "whose writings had done so much to arouse and nourish my mind on tradition" (*T,* vii). However much in sympathy he feels himself with the conservative trend of Eliot's lifelong reflections on tradition, though, Shils is obliged to propose a sociological model of tradition that, in its broadest outlines, differs dramatically from Eliot's notion of tradition in his seminal essay. As a social scientist, Shils proposes the widest possible definition of tradition, based upon the Latin word *traditum* – "anything which is transmitted or handed down from the past to the present" (*T,* 12). This broader conception of tradition diverges most from the normative sort of tradition that Eliot sought to promote throughout his career in that, as Shils says, "The conception of tradition as here understood is silent about whether there is acceptable evidence for the truth of the tradition or whether the tradition is accepted without its validity being established. . . . The decisive criterion is that, having been created through human actions, through thought and imagination, it is handed down from one generation to the next" (*T,* 12). Fleshing out his definition, Shils describes the immense range of *tradita* as encompassing

. . . material objects, beliefs about all sorts of things, images of persons and events, practices and institutions. It includes buildings, monuments, landscapes, sculptures, paintings, books, tools, machines. It includes all that a society of a given time possesses and which already existed when its present possessors came upon it and which is not solely the product of physical processes in the external world or exclusively the result of ecological and physiological necessity. (*T,* 12)

If we apply the definition of tradition proposed by Shils, we must admit that America is saturated with tradition. Shils makes it clear that tradition is the central process of cultural transmission, without which culture would vanish. From the sociological perspective, tradition is an indisputable ingredient in every aspect of our lives. Our placement with respect to tradition, however, as encoded in modern terms like "traditionalism," is another matter. As Shils begins his book by noting, the modern valuation of tradition and the attitude we take toward the past serve to render negligible the prestige of tradition, which in turn undercuts its authorizing function: "The acknowledged normative power of a past practice, arrangement, or belief has become very faint, indeed, it is almost extinguished as an intellectual argument. Correspondingly, the traditionality of a belief, practice, or arrangement offers little resistance to arguments which proceed on the presumption of the efficiency, rationality, expediency, 'up-to-dateness,' or progressiveness of their proposed alternatives" (*T,* 1).

Establishing itself in opposition to tradition, modernity is an international phenomenon, and its antitraditional attitude informs the work of modern poets everywhere. America, though, has made itself so "thoroughly modern" that we can conceive of it as something like the flagship of modernity. Constructed in the Renaissance and launched by the concerted winds of the Reformation and the Enlightenment, America represents a thoroughgoing embodiment of the spirit of antitraditionalism. Americans feel a fundamental distrust of tradition and authority, opposing to them as ultimate values freedom and independence. In doing so, we sacrifice the supportive function that foundational myths supply. Instead of basing our culture on prophets, avatars, or heroes who, like Prometheus, bring divine fire down to mortals, we descend from founding fathers who were, like us, without divine sanction and who gave us a law not grounded in absolutes but addressed to a mediate world and to the necessities of adjudication between countervailing claims of interest.

If we return to the standpoint of Shils's broad definition of tradition, we can see that America partakes not only of European tradition but of traditions drawn from around the world. And as more and more cross-cultural studies are undertaken, the image emerges of America as a world culture, woven of a vast array of traditions. In characterizing the prevailing American attitude toward tradition, however, one might argue that the only privileged tradition is antitraditionalism. This antitraditionalism represents not just another tradition; it renders the grounding or authorizing function of tradition itself problematical. In other words, although it can be argued that America has produced a "tradition of the new," to use Harold Rosenberg's coinage, a major feature of this tradition is an anxiety about groundlessness, which arises as a necessary correlative of antitraditionalism. Within this "tradition," American poets keep asking fundamental questions over and over again, wondering whether it is even possible to be a poet in America when the ultimate authority for writing remains under suspicion.

In the twentieth century, this sort of questioning comes to a head in T. S. Eliot's famous essay "Tradition and the Individual Talent." Habitually defending ourselves against seeing the anxiety this questioning provokes, we have enshrined Eliot's essay as a successful accommodation to tradition rather than recognizing it as a naked plea for such inclusion. If we look directly into the heart of the essay, we can hear anxiety and pathos cry out from the shortest paragraph, whose poignancy is highlighted formally by both its brevity and its self-containment. In this paragraph Eliot depicts the poet's lot in the following terms: "What happens is a continual surrender of himself as he is at the moment to something which is more valuable. The progress of an artist is a continual self-sacrifice, a continual extinction of personality" (SP, 40). For what desired good can the poet be willing to extinguish his own personality and sacrifice the conduct of his present life? For tradition. Without tradition, it seems, an individual identity is without meaning and life is not worth living; in order to obtain the treasure of tradition, one eagerly sacrifices lived experience and the sense of self.

Over against the echoes of religious piety, an acute sense of desperation rings out in Eliot's plea for tradition. Instead of assuming, as so many American writers have tried to do, an Adamic posture of rejoicing in his freedom from the bonds of any anteriority, Eliot, on the contrary, feels imprisoned by the lack of tradition and will resort to any extreme in order to claim belonging. Picturing himself as barred from tradition, as if by social class or lack of providential election, the poet proclaims: "Tradition . . . cannot be inherited, and if you want it you must obtain it by great labour" (SP, 38). On the face of it, this statement might sound as though it is thundered at a student by a stern schoolmaster in frock coat; behind that authoritative mask, however, we can hear a call of tremendous yearning, which disguises its plea in the imperative voice, thereby hoping to guarantee fulfillment. The camouflaged call is a prayer: For those without tradition, please make it possible that through our great, penitential labors we may earn it. Backing up this prayer, the puritan

Eliot adopts a penitential covenant of works, which involves following what he calls "the historical sense" – a willing acquiescence to the "compulsion" to flay himself so relentlessly with "the whole of the literature of Europe from Homer and within it the whole of the literature of his own country [i.e., England!]" that its imprint is branded upon whatever he himself writes – as though, like Melville's Queequeg, he could appropriate European tradition by having it tattooed upon his skin.

The "labour" of "obtaining" tradition (does Eliot, like one of James's arriviste characters, think that having sweated hard enough under the protestant work ethic he now has the right to buy tradition?) requires the disciplined working through, one by one, of the imposing monuments of European culture – picking up and engaging each one deliberately, passionately, responsibly, appropriating it even to the extent of embodying it in translation or imitation. Every poet handles certain texts in this way, but to do so specifically for the purpose of acquiring tradition brings tradition into the *foreground* as a brightly lit, fully accessible object for the appropriation of any person, regardless of her or his *background*. In representing tradition as a series of objects, Eliot occludes from awareness the background function of tradition, its operation as "tacit knowledge" or as hermeneutic "prejudice." In a "traditional" society, one for whom the grounding function of tradition remains substantially intact, tradition works in a way precisely the opposite of that expressed by Eliot: Tradition is not earned but given. The authority or weight of tradition inheres in this background function, through which the great monuments of the culture are seen as expressing with consummate clarity and force the truths that "everyone" feels. At the same time as recognizing the monumentality and sublimity – the inexhaustibility or at times even unapproachability – of the great works of one's tradition, one also feels an inalienable intimacy with these works merely by virtue of having been born into this tradition.[2] When we approach a work from outside our own tradition as if it were a singular figure without a ground, we are able to make little sense of it.

Although misunderstanding is an obvious liability in engaging a work outside one's own tradition, we can mistake such misunderstanding for a surface matter if we ignore its more subtle and pervasive background quality, which is the sensation of strangeness, of not being at home, felt when encountering a work from another tradition. Having voluntarily exiled themselves from the authority of European tradition and yet having existed too briefly or arrived too late to establish a tradition of equal depth, authority, and pervasiveness, Americans occupy an uneasy position, which might be called self-estrangement, an estrangement not from particular works thought of as traditional but from the grounding function of tradition itself. The works of the European tradition, like the works of our own American past, do not hide from us, but our relentless appropriation of them cannot, in a like manner, hide our loss of the background sense of the "weight" of the traditional object in its society; the objects of European tradition join those of our own history as familiar but uncannily weightless. Switching metaphors, Charles Olson, in advice offered to Cid Corman on how to situate his new magazine *Origin* (at a moment in which both poets were setting off on their careers), speaks of this quality of weightlessness as a breathlessness that undercuts the stamina of an American writer:

> Look: any French writer . . . stands on SCHOLARSHIP of his people (as well as a clear tradition back thru the Latin to the Greek and on back)
>
> he can be interlacktuwal as all hell *because* he has a body of work which he and his readers take for granted, base themselves on (a culture breathes, takes breath for granted, as men do)
>
> but such breath has been worked for, millenniums, my lad
>
> DO YOU HONESTLY THINK – or know, for that matter –ANY AMERICAN CAN GO ON SUCH ASSUMPTION?
>
> > Have you *any* sanctions for your acts?
> > *Even* for editing a MAG?[3]

In a similar moment of reflection upon the weightlessness of American culture, the philosopher Stanley Cavell notes the unsanctioned, ephemeral quality of our intellectual life:

> I think a . . . cultural difference between American and European intellectual life is that the American (with isolated exceptions) has no sacred intellectual texts, none whose authority the intellectual community at large is anxious to preserve at all costs – no Marxian texts, no Freudian, no Hegelian, no Deweyan, and so forth. Every text stands at the level of professional journal articles, open for disposal.[4]

The American antipathy to viewing texts as sacred objects, as issues from a primordial ground, accounts for some of the differences in inflection between European and American modernism. The relationship of the writer to tradition in, for example, Joyce's *Ulysses* and Broch's *Death of Virgil* is quite different from that relationship in Pound's *Cantos* and Eliot's *Waste Land*. Through excision or imitation, the Americans assemble pieces of tradition onto a spatially organized plane, which, though infinitely extensible, remains flat; the Europeans mine the temporal layers of tradition as an inexhaustible source for ever new inventions. Eliot seems to have recognized that, without the grounding function of tradition intact, a writer is left with merely the isolate objects of tradition; in "Tradition and the Individual Talent" he creates an image of tradition as an ideal coherence of the individual works within it. By appropriating this ideal coherence, the American poet would gain a substitute for the background sense of tradition as tacit authorization from which he feels exiled – as though by drafting a map one could guarantee a place for oneself. Eliot imagines a tradition that "has a simultaneous existence and composes a simultaneous order," and then he plots out his position within this simultaneity:

> The existing monuments form an ideal order among themselves, which is modified by the introduction of the new (the really new) work of art among them. The existing order is complete before the new work arrives; for order to persist after the supervention of novelty, the *whole* existing order must be, if every so slightly, altered; and so the relations, proportions, values of each work of art toward the whole are readjusted. . . . Whoever has approved of this idea of order, of the form of European, of English literature will not find it preposterous that the past should be altered by the present as much as the present is directed by the past. (*SP*, 38–9)

In this cubist view, tradition is spatialized as a revisable collage, neither temporally grounded nor unalterably fixed, but rather laid out as a simultaneous visual arrangement, capable both of supporting and of being recast by the "really new" work of art. No one will deny that traditions change, but to speak of tradition spatially as a "form," as though it were a modernist work of art, is truly preposterous.[5] Although most people in traditional societies imagine tradition as in important ways unalterable, one might wish to take a historical perspective and imagine it more as a massive inertial force, moving slowly through time, deflected slightly in one direction or another by the addition of a new work of art. Eliot's claim that "the past should be altered by the present as much as the present is directed by the past" represents, not the hermeneutic recognition that our understanding of the past is conditioned by our present perspective, but rather the desire of an exiled American to create his own collage, to call to order himself the ground upon which his new production may securely rest.

"THE PREMISE THAT SERVES TO FIX US FIXES ALSO THAT PART OF THEM WHICH WE REMEMBER"

Evincing an anxiety comparable to Eliot's, William Carlos Williams, too, sought a way to appropriate the past in order to situate himself as a poet. Instead of looking to the monuments of European tradition and to the value of traditionalism, Williams wished to ground himself in the American continent, which meant, in effect, to revise and make his own the record of past attempts by Europeans and their descendants to situate themselves in America. By reconceiving American history, Williams hoped to find himself – in America. Praising Daniel Boone as an exemplary hero, Williams proclaimed, "his whole soul, with greatest devotion, was given to the New World which he adored and found, in its every expression, the land of heart's desire" (*IAG*, 139). Williams, too, in his revisionary history, *In the American Grain,* offers "his whole soul" to reconfiguring American history, looking to find in it somewhere "the land of heart's desire." Through characterizing the fidelity to place of Boone and the other heroes in his select pantheon, such as Columbus, de Soto, Père Sebastian Rasles, John Paul Jones, Aaron Burr, Sam Houston, and Poe, Williams hopes that the positive qualities he uncovers in this unorthodox band of found(l)ing fathers will redound upon himself and give sanction to his own efforts at grounding.

In his imagination, Williams claims a filial descent from the Daniel Boone whom he describes in fabulous terms: "There was, thank God, a great voluptuary born to the American settlements against the niggardliness of the damning puritanical tradition; one who by the single logic of his passion, which he rested on the savage life about him, destroyed at its spring that spiritually withering plague" (*IAG*, 130). Against the notion of Williams as a new Boone, taking his place directly in the "true," voluptuary American lineage, Henry Seidel Canby, in "Back to the Indian," the first review of *In the American Grain,* noted perceptively that Williams's version of "noble savagery" had a Parisian rather than an American flavor. Canby drily portrayed Williams as "an American poet and modernist, who surveys his home from the perspective of Paris," and ended his review by lecturing Williams in terms resembling those of a father reproving his renegade son: "There is undoubtedly much to cause discontent in the spectacle of America as the fatted calf among the nations, but to choose rampageous Indians and political reprobates as ancestral models by way of a change from puritans, Quakers, and Virginia gentlemen is to strike a Parisian attitude which seems a little absurd in New York."[6]

In confirmation of Canby's viewpoint, we can note that *In the American Grain* is the only book that Williams, the staunch "non-expatriate," composed, in large measure, outside the United States. As one critic has argued, "We might even speculate that *In the American Grain* could not have been written in Rutherford, that he required this separation to look carefully at the texture of American culture resident in him. Williams suggested this possibility when he wrote . . . that 'all values have grown much simpler for me since I have hit Paris.' "[7] Although this simplification of values seems to be the object of Canby's scorn, he fails to note that the simple-minded condemnation of puritanism is as much an American peculiarity as puritanism itself. Alert to the issue that Canby raises, Williams records within his text a confrontation with Parisian values that helped to solidify his decidedly American intent in writing *In the American Grain*. As he had done earlier with his quotations from and responses to his fellow poets in "The Return of the Sun," the prologue to *Kora in Hell,* and as he was to do most memorably through the "Cress" letters in *Paterson,* Williams introduced directly into his text the confrontational voice of another speaker – in this case the French writer Valèry Larbaud. Williams allows Larbaud to comment upon the provincialism of Williams's own diatribe against puritanism, and thus he can partially disarm in advance a Canby's criticism. But more importantly, this dialogue functions as a way for Williams to maintain that his central concern is neither with an "objective" history of America nor with a distanced "appreciation" of its conflicting elements (such as Larbaud enjoys) but rather with recuperating particular historical figures whose works and attitudes can supply a groundwork for American culture:

> I said, It is an extraordinary phenomenon that Americans have lost the sense . . . that there is a source in AMERICA for everything we think or do; . . . that, in fine, we have no conception at all of what is meant by moral, since we recognize no ground our own – and that this rudeness rests all upon the unstudied character of our beginnings. . . . That unless everything that is, proclaim a ground on which it stand, it has no worth; and that what has been morally, aesthetically worth while in America has rested upon peculiar and discoverable ground. (*IAG,* 109)

This passage sounds the leitmotifs of the American poetic situation: our inability to recognize ourselves as in possession of a ground; the impulse to begin work as a poet by writing a myth of our beginnings through which we can father (and mother) ourselves; and the apprehension that without a ground to stand on, no cultural work has any worth. In an incomplete understanding of what is at stake in "a ground on which it stand," readers have taken the idiosyncratic American history that Williams composed while on his European sabbatical as a fiercely nativist declaration of the necessity for *contact* between the writer and the continent, "the land of heart's desire." J. Hillis Miller has provided an influential formulation of this aspect of the desire for grounding; he speaks of Williams's search for immanence, in the course of which the heart's desire springs forth out of the "formless ground" of the American landscape.[8] But is Miller's "formless" ground the one Williams has in mind here? In the passage quoted above, Williams decries our formless culture, our rude unstudiedness, and he laments, rather, our lack of "recognizing" a ground, of acknowledging that "there is a source in AMERICA for everything we think or do." The ground Williams yearns for is not primarily that vast, unknown (and thus feminized, in Williams's imagination) continent that opened before the many explorers whom he takes such pains to recharacterize; instead, the ground must be constructed from a historical investigation of the exploratory tradition in which Williams would like to situate himself. The ground is textual, the result of a revisionary reading – a fact Williams hints at by speaking of the ground Boone found "to take the place of England" as "the New World which he adored and found, *in its every expression,* the land of heart's desire [emphasis added]" (*IAG,* 136). As Bryce Conrad notes in his excellent study of *In the American Grain,* Williams conceived of history as a battle of words – a battle between texts that smother individuality and those which arise directly from individual experience:

> Williams' methodology suspends all questions of history's objective existence. There is no innate story or form in the past that one must come to know and in pursuit of which one will of necessity become lost among "mountains of dead words," among "cemeteries of words." . . . Yet it is only the sharp edges of the word itself that can cleave through the mass, the word of the individual who gathers the past "like fruit on a tree." Williams presents a practice clear, simple, radical, and anti-institutional – history "must be put down each for himself, read each for himself."[9]

Through his inscription of an idiosyncratic history, Williams uses *In the American Grain* to construct a grounding for his poetry in a way not unlike that of his ostensible arch-rival, Eliot: Each American poet feels profoundly unsettled and unsupported, and each endeavors to develop a notion of tradition that will underwrite his own poetic enterprise. I would contend that Williams is most "American" neither in his love for the landscape nor in his nativist rhetoric. He may approach that condition, ironically (as so many others have done), by composing his American history abroad, but he actually reaches it, like Eliot and every other major American poet since Emerson, by creating an idiosyncratic history to satisfy his deep longing for a tradition of his own to authorize his poetry.

One way in which it would seem that the "new" tradition Williams assembles for *In the American Grain* differs markedly from the "old" tradition Eliot invokes in "Tradition and the Individual Talent" is that, when Williams considers the "morally, aesthetically worth while" in poetry, only Edgar Allan Poe makes the grade. Poe, as many commentators have remarked, seems a rather odd choice by Williams of literary predecessor (isn't he a member of Eliot's team?); from the standpoint of esthetic principles, Poe the symbolist and Williams the objectivist appear to have little in common. But Williams does not really care about Poe's esthetics, or his style; he is captivated by Poe's acts of situating himself as a writer. Although he *is* intrigued that Poe claims to have written his poems according to a method (thus obtaining a "scientific" grounding), Williams's real concern lies with Poe's criticism: "The aspects of his critical statements as a whole, from their hundred American titles to the inmost structure of his sentences, is that of a single gesture, not avoiding the trivial, to sweep all worthless chaff aside. It is a movement, first and last to clear the GROUND" (*IAG*, 216). Poe becomes Williams's exemplary American poet because he is a violent revisionist, a fierce partisan in the battle for a place to stand; he also admires Poe's tenacity in the search for principles that could ground American writing and in attacking whatever would obscure those principles. In his own reading of Poe, Williams finds himself having to exercise identical virtues in interpreting his subject: "As with all else in America, the value of Poe's genius to OURSELVES must be *uncovered* from our droppings, or at least uncovered from the 'protection' which it must have raised about itself to have survived in any form among us – where everything is quickly trampled" (*IAG*, 219).

The Poe that Williams disclosed – the relentless critic of all shabby, secondhand imposture in European clothing – did provide a kind of ancestral image for Williams's own project of uncovering the grounds for an American tradition. He discerned, for example, that Poe faced factors in the American condition that had not changed materially by Williams's own era; he mentions two factors in particular as impinging upon Poe: "the necessity for a fresh beginning, backed by a native vigor of extraordinary proportions, – with the corollary, that all 'colonial imitation' must be swept aside." Williams would find himself asserting over and over again the necessity for a new "Spring" in American poetry that will express our "native vigor" to the fullest extent; and his disparagement of literary "colonialism" was to occupy a major place in his own critical endeavors. Williams also resembled Poe in that he "saw his own despair . . . , yet he continued to attack, with amazing genius seeking to discover, and discovering, points of firmness by which to STAND and grasp, against the slipping way they had of holding on in his locality." Speaking for both men, Williams proclaims willfully: "Either the New World must be mine as I will have it, or it is a worthless bog. There can be no concession" (*IAG*, 219). A worthless bog is no place to stand.

Had he chosen to read Eliot as he read Poe, Williams might have seen Eliot, too, as a comrade-in-arms, battling anxiety and despair in the revisionary project of clearing away the American ground and making a space available for his own work. All three poets entered the fray armed with little more than self-reliance, seeking to establish a ground that was based upon their own individual judgments; as a revisionist, each poet sought to be "original," as Williams says, "in its legitimate sense of solidity which goes back to the ground, a conviction that he *can* judge within himself" (*IAG*, 216). For the American poet, grounding is necessarily a revisionist enterprise, in which the poet finds him or herself in the awkward position of a latecomer to a European tradition that is both constitutive of and alien to the conditions out of which the poet writes. Although modern European poets inherit similar constraints, the situation in America seems more extreme because no (European) grounding cultural tradition has ever existed here in the first place. Receiving as their primary legacy this double jeopardy of belatedness and alienation, American poets such as Williams and Eliot construct a tradition using the principles of collage, discriminating fiercely among the objects lying at hand and arranging them in a form meant to support their own work.

A major thesis of *In the American Grain* is that each of us must do the primary work of rewriting history. We cannot rely upon what has come down to us, for "if there is agreement on one point in history, be sure there's interest to have it so and that's not truth" (*IAG*, 188). This insistence upon the necessity of finding the truth of history for oneself becomes a central issue for Olson as well, as we shall see in the next chapter, and it has a direct antecedent in the self-reliant philosophy of Emerson.[10] In Williams's terms, a revisionist history will look for the motives responsible for repressing a true account of a person's character and also seek to recover that character:

> We can begin by saying: No opinion can be trusted; even the facts may be nothing but a printer's error; but if a verdict be unanimous, it is sure to be a wrong one, a crude rush of the herd which has carried its object before it like a helpless condoning image. If we cannot make a man live again when he is gone, it is boorish to imprison him dead within some narrow definition, when, were he in his shoes before us, we could not do it. It's lies, such history, and dangerous. Just there may lie our hope for the future, beneath that stone of prejudice. (*IAG*, 190)

Since identity is multifarious, there can never be only one approach to history. Given this understanding, Williams looks for the motives for confining the accounts given of a person's character into a univalent morality play, laying all the blame for such normative historiography at the door of puritanism, which he sees as the contagion at work in the distortion and defamation of strong American characters. While he purports to restore some of the complexity to our understanding of various historical characters, Williams can make, of course, no claim to disinterestedness, since his own motive is to use historical inquiry to provide a ground for his poetry: "That of the dead which exists in our imaginations has as much fact as have we ourselves. The premise that serves to fix us fixes also that part of them which we remember" (*IAG*, 189). There can be no clearer statement on the interdependence of this sort of revisionary history and the poetry it authorizes.

But then Williams himself, afraid that his own history could become a "helpless condoning image," balks at the metaphor of fixity; it seems to belie the multifariousness he endeavors to unleash. How can we choose an authorizing image of a past figure and not fall into the "deadening," "imprisoning" discourse of normative historiography? The only way, says Williams, is by acknowledging the provisional nature of our acts of grounding, by continuing to affirm over and over again that the true purpose of history is to make new creation possible. If history is "as it may be, a tyranny over the souls of the dead – and so the imaginations of the living – where lies our greatest well of inspiration, our greatest hope of freedom (since the future is totally blank, if not black) we should guard it doubly from the interlopers" (*IAG*, 189). When we open up a revisionary history and guard against its appropriation by "interlopers" who wish to reduce it to "some narrow definition," then we have available the cleared ground upon which an American poet can hope to write. When Williams announces this sort of productive history, his imaginary respondent interjects: "You mean, tradition. Yes, nothing there is metaphysical. It is the better part of us all." To which Williams enthusiastically replies, "It is the fountain!" (*IAG*, 189).

In "Tradition and the Individual Talent" and *In the American Grain*, the poets seek to allay their anxiety by constructing idiosyncratic traditions intended to keep the ground for their writing revisable and open. Eliot holds the ground open by imagining a tradition that, instead of disdaining, eagerly awaits the imposition of the new work of art. Williams maintains a hospitable ground by constructing an exploratory tradition of heroic revisionism, one that remains always in the process of clearing away ideological stagnancy. Whether one imagines gaining access to tradition by the penitential gambit of passive surrender or by aggressive intrusion is a matter of personality; more fundamentally, the revisionary traditions constructed by Eliot and Williams function identically as idio-syncratic modes of grounding. And it is important to observe that as soon as either of these encompassing collages of tradition has begun to look like "the" tradition, subsequent American poets have bridled, feel-ing called upon to undertake another revisionary intervention.

"THE OTHERNESS OF TRADITION"

Having seen how Eliot and Williams rolled out tradition as a map, in the hope of locating themselves somewhere within its coordinates, let us return for one more inspection of the notion of tradition and its relation to modernity. In Edward Shils's endeavor to construct a careful so-ciological description of tradition and (between the lines) to argue for the sort of traditionalism he sees embodied in T. S. Eliot, he makes it clear how important the authorizing function of tradition is for the continued production of culture. Through his central definition of tradition as the "given," Shils weds two notions: the objectification of tradition as "things handed down" and the weight of the authority invested in tradi-tion. This conception of tradition as the given only achieves articulation in the modern era, where it emerges in the dissatisfaction (called conser-vative) with the radical rejection of the authority of tradition by the more enthusiastic proponents of modernism. Giving vent to this dissatisfac-tion, Shils tries to distance himself from modernism:

> Modern culture is in some respects a titanic and deliberate effort to
> undo by technology, rationality, and governmental policy the
> givenness of what came down from the past. . . . Archimedes in
> the third century B.C. was not ready to accept the given position of
> the earth in the cosmos; he said, "Give me but one firm spot on
> which to stand, and I will move the earth." No one ever provided
> that firm place or fulcrum to Archimedes and so he had to accept as
> given the position of the earth in the cosmos. Many of the activities
> undertaken by scientists and governmental officials, technologists,
> and psychologists are efforts to create the fulcrum so that they can
> undo, minimize, or annul the influence of what has been given by
> the past to the present. (T, 197–8)

As a conservative modernist, Shils fears the loss of the normative dimen-sion supplied by the givenness of tradition, feeling that the world would be a more pleasant, safer place if we would accept a bit more of what we are given. By his self-conscious emphasis on the concept of givenness, though, he joins both the radical enthusiasts of change and the vast, unself-conscious modernist majority (we complacent adherents to the principle of accelerating change, for whom it appears "natural") in conceiving of tradition as a ragbag of objects one can either accept or reject. From this perspective, Eliot truly does look paradigmatic: as a modernist thinker he recasts tradition into a set of objects juxtaposable into an authorizing collage; as a poet, he writes the great modernist poem, *The Waste Land,* in which he demonstrates how the modern art of poetry creates its own grounding through a collagist reordering of tradition.

From a sociological perspective, one can objectify and enumerate the traditional factors at play within a particular social situation, thus to weigh the influence of tradition and judge the authorizing role that it plays. But does this modernist conception of tradition as "what has been given by the past to the present" exhaust the significance of the term? One might counter the modernist definition by arguing the diametrically opposed position that tradition contains primarily what is withheld by the past from the present. A careful reading of an ancient work of art or writing often discloses a fundamental strangeness, a darkness or hidden-ness that refuses to yield to our normal modes of mastering texts. Along with "giving" what we "take for granted," tradition also guards what we are unable to grasp, whether we call it "death," "fate," "the gods," or "human nature," keeping this ungraspable otherness in close proximity to us. We could conceive of tradition as coming to birth in the moment of confrontation with our groundlessness, with our inability to conceive of or feel at home with a strangeness that intimately concerns us. From this vantage point, what persists in tradition is that which we cannot explain away, for which no interpretation is final, and which never allows us to feel in control; rather than giving, tradition withholds what matters most, and it is the struggle of a lifetime to pry oneself open to an intima-tion of what tradition guards.

If we combine these two definitions and describe tradition as a with-holding in the midst of giving, then we can say that modernity fears to face the unsettling quality in tradition, its posing of questions that threat-en to take away everything that is "given" in our lives, to deprive us of our place. We could think of modernity as an attempt to control tradi-tion: In the form of what Heidegger calls the *Gestell,* the rigid frame of objectification into which it tries to squeeze all that is, modernity flees from the strangeness of tradition, its radically unsettling effect.[11] In a discussion of the inadequacy of our understanding of tradition, Gerald L. Bruns calls this unsettling effect "the otherness of tradition":

> . . . that is, the idea that what comes down to us in tradition, what
> tradition preserves or rather entails, is not a deposit of familiar
> meanings but something strange and refractory to interpretation,
> resistant to the present, uncontainable in the given world in which
> we find ourselves at home, the world that makes sense to us and

promises us a future that has a place for us . . . tradition is not the
persistence of the same; on the contrary, it is the disruption of the
same by that which cannot be repressed or subsumed into a familiar
category.[12]

In the period that we designate as modernism (roughly, from 1890 to
1940), the most far-reaching and consummate attempts were made to
corral the givens of tradition into a national park of culture. The primary
art form of modernism, as David Antin has argued, was the collage – the
"enframing" of a number of disparate given objects – which became a
ubiquitous structural principle in the arts and the human sciences.[13] In
fact, the term "structural principle" itself bespeaks a collagist epistemology. There have been American poets before, after, and even during this
period (such as H.D., Williams to some extent, and even Pound at moments) who have looked behind the modernist drive to frame tradition as
a set of givens that one holds in reserve and marshals for authorization,
writers who have sought to become accountable to what Bruns calls "the
otherness of tradition." Because our critical perspective has been so per-
vasively defined by modernism, we often have difficulty seeing clearly or
taking seriously the less "masterful" orientation toward tradition that one
can find among a number of the transcendentalists, the objectivists, the
projectivists, and the Language poets. In important ways these writers
turn aside from modernity and reinvoke fundamental, disorienting questions that modernism seeks to escape from by foregrounding "technique," dogma, or ideology. These questions require the ethical vulnerability of offering oneself as a site for the apparition of the paradoxical
strangeness of tradition.

Eluding the grasp of modernism, many of the poets in the movements
mentioned above actively cultivate these disorienting questions, setting
forth the poem as a place where the most unexpected confrontations may
occur. In opening the text and precluding mastery, these writers cannot,
however, overlook the modern crisis of authority; we find them continually proposing and overcoming modes of grounding. If the modernist revision of tradition into a set of normative givens reaches its logical
conclusion in the spatialization and formalism of the collage, then something different takes place in the poets who are not so wedded to modernism; projectivist poets, for instance, introduce elements of temporality
and everydayness in such a way as to allow the implicit collagist frame of
modernity to disintegrate and thus to make traditional questions perti-
nent once again. Poets such as Charles Olson, Robert Duncan, Robert
Creeley, Denise Levertov, Paul Blackburn, Edward Dorn, Hilda Morley,
and George Oppen (who reemerged in the sixties) might be fruitfully
characterized as post-collage, highlighting the fact that the hold exercised

by modernist collage begins to dissolve in their writing. Their characteristic poetic strategies for finding but not fixing the ground, like those of Emerson, Thoreau, and Whitman, take clearer cognizance of the paradoxical nature of tradition as simultaneously an authorizing agent and a guardian of the uncontrollable. This dual nature of tradition forms the template for the three paradoxical methods – containment, circling, and repetition – that are discussed in the remainder of this study.

In his most famous meditation upon the hiddenness of tradition, "The Kingfishers," Olson speaks as an "archaeologist of morning," investigating, like Williams, the secrets buried in the earth. Whereas Williams found comfort in figures like Daniel Boone and Edgar Allan Poe, who seemed to authorize his revisionary grounding scheme, Olson confronts the lost meaning of the Omphalos stone at the Delphic oracle and the dark secrets buried in the sacrificial pit in Ancient Mexico, sites where one meets "traditional" questions in their most baffling or frightening immediacy. In "The Kingfishers," Olson thinks about what tradition withholds and about how the present stands with respect to that withholding. The bird itself, so important as a Christian symbol in Eliot's *Four Quartets,* becomes in the opening scene of Olson's poem merely the emblem of a decadent intellectualism: "Fernand, who had talked lispingly of Albers and Angkor Vat . . . could not go beyond his thought / 'The pool the kingfishers' feathers were wealth why / did the export stop?" (*CP,* 86).[14] Olson indicts the intellectual's cultural collage of (Josef) Albers, Angkor Vat (*sic*), Chichen Itza, and the Christian legends of the kingfisher as created by a sterile, essentially defensive reaction against the direct knowledge of otherness that tradition demands. Olson, like Pound (who does not escape censure in the poem for his own refusal to confront the other), turns away from cocktail party banter toward primary research and learns an important fact about the kingfishers – the decomposition at the center of their nurturance:

> It nests at the end of a tunnel bored by itself in a bank. There,
> six or eight white and translucent eggs are laid, on fishbones
> not on bare clay, on bones thrown up in pellets by the birds.
>
> On these rejectamenta
> (as they accumulate they form a cup-shaped structure) the young
>   are born.
> And, as they are fed and grow, this nest of excrement and decayed
>   fish becomes
>   a dripping, fetid mass
>   (*CP,* 87)

Olson's discovery of the biological dependence of the birds upon decay is joined by an investigation of the cultural importance of feathers, which he follows to Prescott's account of the conquest of Mexico by Cortés: as Olson notes, Cortés "tore the eastern idols down, toppled / the temple walls, which, says the excuser / were black from human gore" (*CP*, 91). Williams, too, using Cortés's letters in his chapter "The Destruction of Tenochtitlan," was aware of the feathers (he mourns "a spirit mysterious, constructive, independent, puissant with natural wealth; light, if it may be as feathers; a spirit lost in that soil" [*IAG*, 32]), but he, like Olson, senses a lost link with tradition in the Aztec human sacrifices that were used as a justification for the devastation Cortés wreaked: "Here it was [in the temples] that the tribe's deep feeling for a reality that stems back into the permanent remote origins had its firm hold. It was the earthward thrust of their logic; blood and earth; the realization of their primal and continuous identity with the ground itself, where everything is fixed in darkness" (*IAG*, 33–4). Taking off from Williams's intuition of the earthliness of human sacrifice, Olson links it with cannibalism (reported by Marco Polo) as two instances of the dirt-and-gore-encrusted roots of civilization, the "dripping fetid mass" in which the cultural meets the biological. Remarking "with what violence benevolence is bought," Olson expresses disgust at this frighteningly destructive aspect of human culture, but he refuses to gloss it over: In the age of Auschwitz and Hiroshima (the poem was written in 1949), how could he? The Aztec and Mayan sacrificial practices, like the maddeningly enigmatic "E" on the stone at Delphi, signal the absolute recalcitrance of tradition, which gives us intimations of unbearably profound meanings and challenges us to a lifetime of investigation in search of what it withholds. For both Olson and Williams, the earth is the image of that withholding, which Olson vows to investigate by quoting from a previous "archeologist," Rimbaud: "si j'ai du goût, ce n'est guères / que pour la terre et les pierres" (*CP*, 92).[15] While sharpening his taste on earth and stones, Olson works a variation on Rimbaud's lines, in order to show how his archeological investigations will mine the same traditional ground: "if I have any taste / it is only because I have interested myself / in what was slain in the sun" (*CP*, 92–3). And then he ends the poem by choosing one notion of tradition over another:

> I pose you your question:
> shall you uncover honey / where maggots are?
> I hung among stones   (*CP*, 93)[16]

Finding at this late day the honey of European tradition infested with maggots, Olson looks to the American earth to provide a more concrete and healthy, if more enigmatic, grounding.

In the most influential essay on "The Kingfishers," Guy Davenport relates it directly to modernism by calling it an "ideogram": "the poem, like a canto of Pound, is a single ideogram, its components working in synergy." Sherman Paul, following in Davenport's footsteps, takes for granted the ideogrammic quality of the poem, commenting, "Ideogram is collage." And Laszlo Géfin, in *Ideogram: History of a Poetic Method,* devotes a chapter to Olson as a practitioner in the "ideogrammic tradition within modern American poetry."[17] Olson's appropriation of Fenollosa's essay *The Chinese Written Character as a Medium for Poetry* and his inheritance from and rebellion against Ezra Pound are complex subjects, which in fact give rise to many of the issues in "The Kingfishers." Rather than consider these matters, though, I would like to contend that something new happens in "The Kingfishers" and its companion poem, "The Praises": Olson begins to break up the Poundian ideogram.[18] Instead of "gathering from the air a live tradition" and binding it into an ideogram, Olson begins to loosen the grasp of appropriation and makes himself responsible to the stony demands lurking within an "earth" of tradition (which he comes to call "an actual earth of value" [*Max,* 584]). Like one of Pound's cantos, "The Kingfishers" consists of many short poetic units, whose continuity with one another can be hard to detect. In most of Pound's cantos, however, a centripetal force draws the disparate elements of the poem toward one or two central principles. The units of Olson's poems often look outward rather than inward; Olson's restless gestures continually break through conceptual frames in an effort to lay himself open to the recalcitrant mysteries he seeks to interrogate rather than appropriate.

Like Williams and Eliot, Olson looks for authorization by constructing an idiosyncratic tradition; *Call Me Ishmael,* for example, might be mistaken for an expanded chapter of *In the American Grain.* Alongside this instrumental relationship toward tradition, Olson also attempts to hold himself accountable to the otherness of tradition in a way that Eliot seemed reluctant even to imagine. Williams, on the other hand, did prepare the way for Olson and others back to this mysterious tradition that partakes of both the chthonic and the celestial; but Williams, like Eliot, remains to a large extent trapped within the modernist definition of tradition, in which the poet can only work with what is given. Olson, one senses, is trying to wrest forth something that has remained hidden a long time, something whose emergence would profoundly disturb the modern world. Of course, the modern world is already, in its own way, profoundly disturbed. Olson evokes a disturbance that promises a way out of the menacing frame of inevitable disaster within which the modern world chooses to live.

Robert Duncan, too, welcomes the otherness of tradition into his poetry, calling it, in the introduction to *Bending the Bow,* "It":

> In the poem this very lighted room is dark, and the dark alight with love's intentions. *It* is striving to come into existence in these

things, or, all striving to come into existence is It – in this realm of men's languages a poetry of all poetries, *grand collage,* I name It, having only the immediate event of words to speak for It. In the room we, aware or unaware, are the event of ourselves in It. (*BB,* vii)

For Duncan, love is a witness to this otherness ("It" echoes the Freudian "Id"), and its expression in poetry involves him immediately in "a poetry of all poetries," a living tradition that he names "grand collage." Duncan's "grand collage" is an image for poetry as an assembly that can never be framed, a whole whose boundaries are ever fluid. Using Gertrude Stein's notion of "composition" as another way to open up the modernist collage, Duncan remarks:

But now the Composition and we too are never finished, centered, perfected. We are in motion and our meaning lies not in some last or lasting judgment, in some evolution or dialectic toward a higher force or consciousness, but in the content of the whole of us as Adam – the totality of mankind's experience in which our moment, this vision of universal possibility, plays its part; and beyond, the totality of life experience in which Man plays His part, not central, but in every living moment creating a new crisis in the equilibrium of the whole.[19]

Duncan resolves to relinquish control of the "composition," the "grand collage," of his poetry because, in his sense of tradition, otherness is not a threat but rather a constitutive part, and he dares to ask for authorization for his poetry not only from the given but also from the withheld.

Chapter 2

FINDING OUT FOR ONESELF

"FACE TO FACE TO A FACT"

In 1846, "desirous to recover the long lost bottom of Walden Pond," Thoreau devised a practical method to sound it. He lay on the winter ice "with a cod-line and a stone weighing about a pound and a half, and could tell accurately when the stone left the bottom, by having to pull so much harder before the water got underneath to help me. The greatest depth was exactly one hundred and two feet. . . ." By "recovering" Walden's long-lost bottom Thoreau hoped to lay to rest the "many stories told about the bottom, or rather no bottom, of this pond, which certainly had no foundation for themselves. It is remarkable how long men will believe in the bottomlessness of a pond without taking the trouble to sound it." Once he locates the actual bottom of the pond and can assure his "readers that Walden has a reasonably tight bottom at a not unreasonable, though at an unusual, depth," then Thoreau makes a seeming about-face. He wonders: "What if all ponds were shallow? Would it not react on the minds of men? I am thankful that this pond was made deep and pure for a symbol. While men believe in the infinite some ponds will be thought to be bottomless" (*W,* 189).

What is an American writer such as Thoreau seeking when he or she looks for a bottomless bottom? Essentially, this is an issue of grounding, an attempt to authorize the activities of writing and living when one inhabits a culture that has lost the grounding of inherited tradition. The lack of grounding both evokes a characteristic existential anguish in our poets and results in characteristic strategies for overcoming such a void. Although the contemporary projectivist poet Charles Olson never described Thoreau as a significant precursor, their approaches to the question of groundlessness are in certain respects remarkably similar. To compensate for the lack of tradition, these two, like a number of American writers, propose a rootedness in the present moment; Thoreau and

26

Olson can be distinguished from other writers by their use of the method I call "containment" for achieving this type of alternative grounding. In this chapter and the two that follow, Thoreau occupies the background and Olson the foreground for a discussion of containment as a grounding method for American poets.

In a challenging treatment of Thoreau's sounding of Walden Pond, Walter Benn Michaels takes up the passage quoted above as paradigmatic of the myriad unsettling contradictions lurking within Walden:

> Thus, the passage introduces two not entirely complementary sets of dichotomies. In the first, the virtues of a pond with a "tight bottom" are contrasted with the folly of believing in bottomless ponds. But then the terms shift: the tight bottom metamorphoses into the merely "shallow" and the bottomless becomes "the infinite." The hierarchies are inverted here: on the one hand, a "tight bottom" is clearly preferable to delusory bottomlessness, on the other hand, the merely "shallow" is clearly not so good as the symbolically suggestive "infinite."[1]

As Michaels presents it, Thoreau's discussion of plumbing the depths of Walden Pond contains a logical contradiction in its profession of values: we wonder, does Thoreau favor the tight bottom or does he favor bottomlessness? In the course of his article, Michaels adduces a number of such contradictions at different levels of the text in order to make a large critical point: that Walden is an inherently contradictory text, which cannot be reduced to unity without ignoring its basic nature. He takes earlier critics to task for seeking to compel its contradictions into an ironic formal pattern:

> Where nineteenth-century critics tended to regard Walden as an anthology of spectacular fragments and to explain it in terms of the brilliant but disordered personality of its author . . . , more recent criticism, by focusing directly on the art of Walden, has tended to emphasize the rhetorical power of its "paradoxes," finding elegant formal patterns in what were once thought to be mere haphazard blunders. Thus, in accepting unity and coherence not simply as desiderata but as characteristic identifying marks of the work of art, these critics have begun by answering the question I should like to begin asking, the question of Walden's contradictions. (Michaels, 133–4)

There are many ways, though, to ask the question of Walden's contradictions. Michaels's way assumes that Thoreau is urging upon us the necessity of specific moral decisions and then subverting our ability to make those decisions, that Thoreau creates what appear to be clear hierarchies of values – such as seems the case in his preference for a locatable bottom over an illusory bottomlessness — and then promptly undermines each hierarchy, leaving us in a condition of undecidability. Opting for undecidability seems a way of respecting inherent contradictions by not resolving them out of existence, but "undecidability" as a final critical resting place runs the risk of becoming the basis of another reductive interpretation, particularly in the case of Thoreau. Rather than pleading for structural coherence or irreducible undecidability, I would like to view this sort of contradiction in *Walden* as a way of handling the American poetic obsession with foundations, which Thoreau, like many poets, finds himself incapable of treating except through contradiction and paradox.

The centrality in *Walden* of this obsession is even more apparent at the end of "Where I Lived and What I Lived For." Speaking with greater urgency about the desirability of a hard bottom, Thoreau exhorts:

> Let us settle ourselves, and work and wedge our feet downward through the mud and slush of opinion, and prejudice, and tradition, and delusion, and appearance, that alluvion which covers the globe, through Paris and London, through New York and Boston and Concord, through church and state, through poetry and philosophy and religion, till we come to a hard bottom and rocks in place, which we can call *reality,* and say, This is, and no mistake; and then begin, having a *point d'appui, . . .* a place where you might found a wall or a state, or set a lamppost safely. . . . If you stand right fronting and face to face to a fact, you will see the sun glimmer on both its surfaces, as if it were a cimeter, and feel its sweet edge dividing you through the heart and marrow, and so you will happily conclude your mortal career. (*W,* 66)

In this passage, as in the one quoted previously, Thoreau starts out by insisting upon the need for a hard bottom, only to end up by offering the inverted bottomlessness of transcendence. Thinking of the two passages side by side, though, we can discern a narrative quality about them that places logically contradictory notions into a sensible sequence. The sequence runs something like this: first we must work our way down past all of the hearsay notions we have inherited from our neighbors (such as the superstition that Walden is bottomless) and find out the facts for ourselves (for example, plumb Walden to ascertain its 102-foot depth); once we have accomplished this arduous act of discovery or revision, then we find that the facts disclosed through our experiential discipline become endlessly productive (bottomless). This process can be pictured as an hourglass: the attention is first narrowed down and refined until it focuses upon a single fact; at that point of maximum concentration, a transformation occurs that opens up to ever-widening implication.

Like Socrates and Emerson, Thoreau aims his contempt at the unexamined notions we receive from others, proposing in place of hearsay a discipline of attentive perception informed by self-examination. In this light, he prizes Walden Pond for its powers as a reflecting device that aids him in self-penetration; in "The Ponds" he identifies it as eye, mirror, and gem. Alternatively, though, in that chapter he also calls it an original fountain and a pure source. Rather than contradicting the notion of reflection, the image of the pond as self-generating source supplements it by representing the process of self-examination both as endless and as, in some senses, originating that which it discovers.

For Thoreau, the discipline of self-examination involves watching ourselves encounter the world, and it must be performed with one eye turned inward and the other aimed at a clear apprehension of what is before us – that "objective" world that American writers have called "the facts." Although attention to the facts informs the utilitarian bent of American culture, our writers take the facts beyond the realm of utility. In common usage, the term *fact* connotes something that is self-evident; for our writers, the "self-evident" is that which obscures a true apprehension of the fact: a fact is an object for investigation. In seeking to know the facts as fully as possible, American poets open themselves to revising prior conclusions, to using the facts as tools for uncovering new understandings. Thoreau asserts that once we offer ourselves wholeheartedly to the facts, screw up the courage necessary to meet them face-to-face, we find that our previous self-conception is vulnerable and that it must yield to the knife-edge of the things before us. When the facts overwhelm our defenses, they break the bonds of our enclosed "mortality," opening us to bottomlessness. Emerson, too, speaks mysteriously of "the true nectar, which is the ravishment of the intellect by coming nearer to the fact" ("The Poet," *RWE*, 319). For both writers this direct confrontation with arduously achieved facts not only overwhelms our settled conceptions (the false ground of our complacency), it also acts as a nectar or tonic that rejuvenates. As Thoreau counsels, "We need the tonic of wildness" to force us to venture beyond our domestic opinions. "At the same time that we are earnest to explore and learn all things, we require that all things be mysterious and unexplorable. . . . We must be refreshed by the sight of inexhaustible vigor, vast and Titanic features, the sea-coast with its wrecks, the wilderness with its living and its decaying trees, the thunder cloud, and the rain which lasts three weeks and produces freshets. We need to witness our own limits transgressed . . . " (*W*, 209–10). Domesticated facts become for us "creatures of habit," but "wild" facts, arrived at through an arduous quest of discovery, break through the habitual enclosures by which we control the world and ourselves; "the tonic of wildness" administered by facts can render both the world and ourselves mysterious and strange.

By recognizing that the way out of our hidebound ignorance, our sleep within the pseudotradition of hearsay, proceeds through an original exploration of "facts" – which can, in their turn, acquaint us with a boundless mystery – Thoreau demonstrates the necessary interdependence of two of the most salient, though seemingly contradictory, inclinations in American poetry: objectivism and transcendentalism.[2] Although these two terms name particular poetic movements, the names are useful for designating, respectively, the worship of facts, the ordinary, the pragmatic, the tangible, and the equally pervasive yearning for mystery, intuition, and wholeness. In works such as Emerson's *Nature,* Dickinson's poetry, Melville's *Moby-Dick,* Whitman's *Leaves of Grass,* Hemingway's *In Our Time,* Lorine Niedecker's poetry, Williams's *Paterson,* Levertov's early collections, and Olson's *Maximus Poems,* we find a combination of the tough-minded and the mysterious, a reliance upon facts as the legitimate vehicle for glimpses of the bottomless. Throughout *Walden,* objectivism and transcendentalism cooperate as complementary impulses. This paradoxical sounding of facts substitutes a solitary inquiry, conducted by a specially prepared investigator, for the communal authority of a grounding tradition.

"ONE SATURATION JOB"

When Thoreau fronts the fact steadily until it flashes forth and penetrates the heart, he experiences moments of endlessly generative insight, such as occur in his description of Walden Pond in "The Ponds" and in his meditation, in "Spring," upon the sandbank as a demonstration of the principles of growth and form in nature and language. Thoreau's striking enactment of this discipline in *Walden* can be taken as a paradigm for its pursuit in a whole range of American writers, such as Charles Olson, likewise of Massachusetts, who inculcates the same discipline in his student, Ed Dorn, in "A Bibliography on America for Ed Dorn." Like Thoreau, Olson insists that the poet's relation to facts necessitates investigations that have normally been assigned to other explorers, such as the geographer, the anthropologist, the archaeologist, and the historian.[3] In his very active "bibliography," Olson conceives of scholarship as an opportunity for visionary fact-finding; he counsels direct engagement with "PRIMARY DOCUMENTS. And to hook on here is a lifetime of assiduity. Best thing to do is *to dig one thing or place or man* until you yourself know more abt that than is possible to any other man. It doesn't matter whether it's Barbed Wire or Pemmican or Paterson or Iowa. But *exhaust* it. Saturate it. Beat it. / And then u KNOW everything else very fast: one saturation job (it might take 14 years). And you're in, forever." Further on in the letter, Olson returns to this issue: "all goes back to the ONE JOB –

that's where one's nose is whittled. If you don't do that one, you can never do the others. / And it's crazy, how *one* yields" (*AP*, 11–12). Applying Olson's terms to Thoreau, we could say that Thoreau's many years exploring Walden Pond constitute his "saturation job"; the two years recorded in *Walden* represent his attempt to "beat it," based upon his conviction that if he can truly know the facts about Walden Pond, in every season and mood, he will be "in, forever." An interrogation of the Concord area, like one of Gloucester or Paterson, promises a firm foundation that "yields" bottomlessly.

Olson and Thoreau agree upon the hermeneutical necessity of finding things out for oneself. Olson nominates history as the primary discipline of such finding; he represents history as a measuring of human possibility, in which the intelligence of the measurer is as crucial as the evidence to be measured. Just as Thoreau prides himself upon his neat solution to the problem of measuring the depth of Walden Pond, Olson exults throughout *The Maximus Poems* in the moments when he discovers a measure for scholarly facts that yields a new insight into human possibility. Olson shares with another original Massachusetts historian, Henry Adams, this view of history as a gauging of human possibility in which the measurer must be taken into account. Olson also concurs with Adams in the conviction that a true education will prepare one to act with assurance in the present moment; both find the ultimate purpose of historical wisdom in the readiness to seize the moment rather than in the safer activity of analyzing the past. Placing himself more specifically in accord with Thoreau, Olson bases his notion of history as a discipline upon the distinction between accepting hearsay and conducting one's own investigation. Taking the first Greek historian, Herodotus, as his model, Olson claims that " 'istorin in him appears to mean 'finding out for oneself,' instead of depending upon hearsay. The word had already been used by the philosophers. 'But while they were looking for truth, Herodotus is looking for the evidence' " (*SVH*, 20).[4] Assuming the mantle of the fact-finding historian in *The Maximus Poems*, Olson professes:

> I would be an historian as Herodotus was, looking
> for oneself for the evidence of
> what is said . . .   (*Max*, 104–5)

Thoreau, too, was a revisionary historian, going against the grain of the evolutionary historical narratives being written in the nineteenth century. Whereas most historians endeavored to present the "rise of civilization" in such a way as to justify the American expansion and domination of territory, Thoreau wrote a "natural history" that placed "civilized" history into the context of the nature and native peoples of North America. Joan Burbick calls Thoreau's history "uncivil": "Splitting history into 'civil' and 'uncivil' accounts, Thoreau aligns himself with wildness and incivility and writes a record of the past that implicitly dismantles the texts of the romantic or civil historian and casts doubt over the story of the American nation."[5] Sherman Paul also discusses the historical aspect of Thoreau's natural history, noting how his conception of it answers directly to the kind of experiential "field work" that Olson proposes for himself as historian:

> The field work involved in writing natural history is a discipline of *hewing to experience* [in Olson's terms], is literally grounded in nature, in the fact of geography. It involves the disposition, the concern with one's immediate life and references, that Olson, a walker like Thoreau, called "human business"; it is notable for its intimacy, its familiarity. It is always a present activity of discovery, always particularist, more readily serving myth and the allegory of the self than generalization.[6]

In *The Special View of History,* a series of lectures given at Black Mountain College in 1956, Olson elaborates in great detail upon history as a discipline for grounding. His notion of history builds upon, but then diverges rather widely from, the academic discipline in which he was trained at Harvard. Not content to research and interpret facts, Olson insists that his job as a historian includes registering his own recognitions of how facts open up to mystery. His unorthodox view of history proceeds even further: in a striking reversal of the nineteenth-century despair provoked by the intrusion of history into religion, Olson feels that history is the only valid ground of belief:

> As much as all imagination does cluster around fiction, it is also true that all belief does cluster around another form of story, history. . . .
>
> By history I mean to know, to really know. The rhyme is still "mystery." We can't stand it. Nothing must be left undone. . . . Even to know that one can't know. Which is the hooker.
>
> . . . one of the uncleannesses of the present is the misapplication of counsel of ritual, an unfortunate tendency of interest to the "Mysteries" instead of, first, a restoration of the principle of fact, which said same "Mysteries" were tough instructors in. . . . I cannot begin to indicate what history is if the dimension of fact as the place of the cluster of belief isn't understood to be the heart of it. (*SVH,* 20–21)[7]

Again, as we saw with Thoreau, the fact opens up to the mystery. The first step away from inaccurate knowledge, sentimental nostalgia, or un-informed belief consists in finding out the facts for oneself. History is knowing something in your bones: "By history I mean to know, to really know." Both Thoreau and Olson testify that the scrupulous, unrelenting pursuit of the facts ("Nothing must be left undone") will deliver one into a proper relation to the bottomless. True history involves a perspective on the world in which one is not "mystified" by the abstract language of academic or bureaucratic hearsay; instead, there is a more active encoun-ter, in which all knowledge is chosen and investigated by a subject con-stantly at risk in the face of what is discovered. "History" is Olson's term for a stance toward life, a stance one acquires by forging against the philosophical grain of Western culture, against that mode of knowledge that depends upon the discourse of general categories, which Olson sees as a species of metaphysical hearsay: "We have had no essential history for two and a half millenia [sic] because the supernatural as well as the natural has been removed from it (by discourse, again, I am sorry to have to repeat, but it is no dead horse I am beating, discourse is still the trammel most of us are caught in and hindered by)" (*SVH*, 23–24).

In his treatment of the supernatural, Olson stands in the romantic line of Blake, Whitman, and Nietzsche, for whom the gods are images of human capacities; this view of the cosmic dimensions of human action was confirmed philosophically by Olson's first reading of Whitehead's *Process and Reality*. In *The Special View of History*, Olson offers an ex-panded model of history, in which both the supernatural and the natural display their ultimate importance as images for individual people to in-habit. This sort of history attends first to the particular and the local and places primary value upon individuals and small communities. Olson advocates this factual supernaturalism as an antidote to the profound alienation in Western culture that results in an ever-diminishing human capacity. Referring to a quotation from Heraclitus, "Man is estranged from that with which he is most familiar" (*SVH*, 14), in which he locates the ancient inception of alienation, Olson propounds a new sense of history:

[Man] either gets his time and place out of himself or via that trope of himself he calls God, and it is the vertu of history as it can now be understood that it restores God as well as locality, and in so doing rids us of two other phonies of discourse, the infinite and the eternal which diluted Him in distracting man from that with which he is necessarily most familiar – what he is. . . . In the end, when all the estrangement is over, when the familiar is known, who isn't up against the face of God like a wall or a mirror where the shadow or the cut-out shape or the light is the reflection or the light or the figure of himself in species? (*SVH*, 25–26)

Eschewing, as an objectivist, totalizing terms like "infinity" and "eternity," Olson arrives, in the final sentence above, at a vision of the fact that sounds remarkably similar to Thoreau's sharp scimitar, whose surfaces reflect the glare of the sun. Both writers claim that an unswerving attention to the local phenomenon yields an experience of the light of divinity, a discovery that cannot be won without the fronting of one's own outline against the light. In an allusion to the figure of Maximus as he develops it in *The Maximus Poems,* Olson hints that the silhouette thrown by the light becomes an image of the human species, like the gnostic image of a composite Person or Hermaphrodite, the primal human writ large. In other words, through a courageous exposure to this light that one releases from the local facts, one can become what Emerson would call a "representative man."[8]

Olson and Thoreau use the epistemological imperative that one find out the facts for oneself as a primary approach to the problem of groundlessness, an approach that can be adopted as spiritual discipline, as political program, and as poetics. As a spiritual discipline, this method sends the initiate (" *'istor* equals *to know,* and *initia* means to begin to find out" [*SVH*, 21]) on a journey from the egotistical surface of what Thoreau calls "gossip" to a bottomless sense of self as founded on inexhaustible mystery. As a political program, it proposes that an individual who locates the true facts of his or her own condition can be of tremendous use to the community as a resistant factor, sustaining the value of the local and the actual against the state, the universal, and the eternal; in Thoreau's terms, this is the politics of being a "neighbor." As a poetics, this approach encourages both the visionary practice of recognizing principles or laws within actual facts and the formal practice of building artistic wholes from an organic series of such recognitions.

"THE ATTENTION, AND / THE CARE"

As an act of situating, the spiritual discipline advocated by Olson and Thoreau places the individual in a particular relation to the outside world. Disregarding the call of an unearthly divinity, these writers pursue a regimen of austerity that can, they claim, bring them into accord, not with the beyond, but with the extensive world itself. In his version of the bottom/bottomless paradox, Olson, like Thoreau, insists upon the irreversible order of containment and extension: extension by itself is pernicious, like the superstition that Walden is a bottomless pond; true extension, the ability to be situated anywhere, is granted only by containment. Using a notion from Keats, Olson views undisciplined extension as "the Egotistical Sublime," an infertile projection of one's small self upon the world, and he connects it with the will to power (*SVH*, 45).[9] When Olson speaks approvingly of "projective size," he considers it a matter of obedience rather than of self-assertion (*SVH*, 45) and specifies that it must arise from containment:

> the use of a man, by himself and thus by others, lies in how he conceives of his relation to nature, that force to which he owes his somewhat small existence. If he sprawl, he shall find little to sing but himself, and shall sing, nature has such paradoxical ways, by way of artificial forms outside himself. But if he stays inside himself, if he is contained within his nature as he is participant in the larger force, he will be able to listen, and his hearing through himself will give him secrets objects share. (*SW*, 25)

In the same essay, "Projective Verse," Olson maintains that a poet cannot be "contained within his nature" and participate in "the larger force" when hampered by "the lyrical interference of the individual as ego." For Olson, the ego is an unbounded subjectivity that "sprawls" across the world, screening from view everything else but itself. Calling it both "subject" and "ego," Olson also refers to this visionary obstruction as the "soul" – "that peculiar presumption by which western man has interposed himself between what he is as a creature of nature (with certain instructions to carry out) and those other creations of nature which we may, with no derogation, call objects" (*SW*, 24). When the ego is contained, the projective poet can, Olson claims, restore a kind of parity between the self and the world; from this position of parity the poet discovers an expansive language that Olson predicts will be able to signify on a scale not just lyric but dramatic or epic (*SW*, 24–26).

In the first of *The Maximus Poems*, "I, Maximus of Gloucester, to You," Olson uses the uncharacteristically feminine image of a nest to figure a containment that dwells in the actual things of one's world. This image occurs right at the outset and is then referred to and amplified throughout the poem. "The thing you're after," counsels Maximus, "may lie around the bend / of the nest" (*Max*, 5).[10] Close at hand, among the things of daily life, lies the key to effective action. As *The Maximus Poems* go on to contend, we can construct, from the particular experiences of each individual and each community, a nest that will, on the one hand, protect us from the false values (such as capitalism, consumerism, nationalism, and universal religion) that abstract us from our own conditions, and will, on the other, give us a purchase upon the grandeur of a more elemental, rooted humanity. And this supportive

enclosure must, Olson insists, be woven of our own particulars, of the
things we find out for ourselves:

> feather to feather added
> (and what is mineral, what
> is curling hair, the string
> you carry in your nervous beak, these
>
> make bulk, these, in the end, are
> the sum   (*Max,* 5)

On the basis, then, of this firm though self-constructed foundation
arises a force that Olson characterizes as phallic, a projective or generative
energy, like a mast arising from a sound hull. When we create a working
foundation through containment, then what issues from this foundation
bears an earned integrity:

> in! in! the bow-sprit, bird, the beak
> in, the bend is, in, goes in, the form
> that which you make, what holds, which is
> the law of object, strut after strut, what you are, what you must be,
>   what
> the force can throw up, can, right now hereinafter erect,
> the mast, the mast, the tender
> mast!   (*Max,* 8)[11]

A slightly different view of containment, as limitation, also appears in
the opening pages of *The Maximus Poems* and complements that of the
nest of particulars. Speaking more directly in "Letter 5" to Vincent Ferrini, the putative addressee of the first run of *Maximus* poems, Olson
deems it unlikely that the citizens of Gloucester will be concerned with,
or even read, Ferrini's new literary magazine:

> . . . This quarterly
> will not be read
>
> The habit of newsprint
> (plus possibly the National Geographic)
> are the limits of
> literacy   (*Max,* 21)

At first this statement strikes one as problematic, for it seems to render
literature and the people of Gloucester mutually incommensurable. Such
an admission would destroy the very premise upon which Olson under-

took to write *The Maximus Poems*: that Gloucester and its people provide
the most exact measure possible for an epic poem. Very quickly Olson
recuperates by setting the limited literacy of Gloucester in another light
than that of lowbrow ignorance:

> I am not at all aware
> that anything more than that
> is called for. Limits
> are what any of us
> are inside of   (*Max,* 21)

By recognizing that limits apply to everyone, that no one commands
an infinite horizon, Olson reinstates an experiential congruence between
his townspeople and himself, in which the work of Gloucester's fishermen stands equivalent to that of Gloucester's poet. As much as Olson
does not wish to raise the people of Gloucester to a hypothetical and
inappropriate level of connoisseurship, making fun of this approach:

> And there is nothing less applicable
> than the complaints of the culture mongers
> about what the people don't know but oh!
> how beautiful they are, how infinite!
> And think how it will be when   (*Max* 22)

he is also aware of the possible trivial and even pernicious activities of the
poet, who may be more captivated by the jingling quality of words and
by the desire to tell entertaining stories than by doing honest work:

> (o Statue,
> o Republic, o
> Tell-A-Vision, the best
> is soap. The true troubadours
> are CBS. Melopoeia
>
> > is for Cokes by Cokes out of
> > Pause
>
>   1V
> (o Po-ets, you
> should getta
> job   (*Max,* 75)

Everyone works; a poet has no special privileges but must attend to
limitations and responsibilities like anyone else. Olson makes a point of

demonstrating, through fishing anecdotes told at this own expense, that
he was incapable of becoming a first-rate fisherman. By this demonstration, he underlines the equivalent challenges waiting for those engaged in
any constructive work; anyone deserves respect who works intelligently
from within realistically apprehended limits:

> Eyes,
> & polis,
> fishermen,
> & poets
>   or in every human head I've known is
>   busy
> both:
> the attention, and
> the care
>   however much each of us
>   chooses our own
>   kin and
>   concentration   (*Max*, 32)

When we practice attention and care toward the limits that define us,
we become productive people. In Olson's mind, what debilitates is not
the lack of one or another hypothetical good, such as literary taste or a
knack for seamanship, but the sense of inadequacy, of dissatisfaction with
what one is. One exercises containment not by measuring oneself against
an external standard but rather by learning to recognize and utilize
oneself more and more fully. By recognizing and respecting our limits,
we come to know ourselves as what we always were. Olson said he
agreed with Edward Dahlberg that

>   . . . people
>
> don't change. They only stand more
> revealed. I,
> likewise   (*Max*, 9)[12]

In speaking of such revelation as a revisionary digging into facts that have
been occluded, Olson wants to combat the pervasive American belief in
unlimited possibilities – which arises, in turn, from dissatisfaction. Acting on this tempting belief, we waste our lives and lay waste the earth.
Expressing concern in his writing for both the earth and our frustrated
lives, Olson seeks to propel us in the opposite direction from the destructive contemplation of unlimited possibilities: only within our own limita-

tions, contained within our own conditions, resides the key to what is truly possible; only through such sustained historical probing do we receive a revelation that is good for us.

Robert Creeley gives testimony to this salutary effect of Olson's insistence upon limits, and to the difficulty of following such a discipline of containment, in the following statement:

> I mistook, I think, the meaning of "freely to write what one chooses," which both de Gourmont and Pound may well have had in mind, because I took "freely" to mean "without significant limit" and "chooses" to be an act of will. I therefore was slow in realizing the nature of Olson's proposal, that "Limits / are what any of us / are inside of," just that I had taken such "limits" to be a frustration of possibility rather than the literal possibility they in fact must provoke. (QG, 71)

Containment "frees" by offering a kind of psychological certainty that is based upon investigating one's own conditions. The American poet confronts, not an Adamic virgin world or self, but an always historically dense external and internal landscape, whose conditions, as Emerson pointed out in "The Poet," provide the true possibilities for our poetic discourse.

"A CERTAIN DOUBLENESS BY WHICH I STAND AS REMOTE FROM MYSELF AS FROM ANOTHER"

Although each "Root person in root place" (Max, 16) is a limited entity, Thoreau, like Olson, stresses that by accepting such containment we avail ourselves of a much greater potential for representing truth. Characteristically, in American writing, the effort to *become* rooted has involved the writer in autobiography, as though learning to speak for oneself were a necessary condition of speaking for, or even with, other Americans. From the Puritan historians through Edwards and Franklin, Adams and Jefferson, Emerson and Thoreau and Douglass and Whitman and Dickinson, Henry James and Henry Adams, and into every corner in the twentieth century, American writers have sought to ground the authority for their pronouncements about America through their scrupulous containment in acts of self-exploration. According to Thoreau, this autobiographical containment avoids hearsay and yields a firm foundation for discourse with other people:

> In most books, the *I*, or first person, is omitted; in this it will be retained. . . . We commonly do not remember that it is, after all,

always the first person that is speaking. I should not talk so much about myself if there were any body else whom I knew as well. Unfortunately, I am confined to this theme by the narrowness of my experience. Moreover, I, on my side, require of every writer, first or last, a simple and sincere account of his own life, and not merely what he has heard of other men's lives. (*W*, 1)

Drily lamenting his containment within the autobiographical – "Unfortunately, I am confined to this theme by the narrowness of my experience" – Thoreau contends that everyone, of course, is in the same predicament. Few of us, however, have the courage to base our lives, not upon a ready-made identity bestowed by society, but rather upon our own self-explorations. In a lecture that meditates in detail upon the implications of an autobiographical perspective toward knowledge and action, Robert Creeley specifies the "hearsay" quality of a generalized identity: "There was, sadly, a professor employed at the University of New Mexico who one time began a lecture with the statement: As I was shaving this morning, seeing myself in the mirror, Professor Jones, I said . . . That is the end of the story, just another professor, no one otherwise home."[13] We dream of the security promised by such a stable, reliable identity. Creeley, like Thoreau, seeks to wake us up by asking: "Why not speak for yourself. Sooner or later you'll have to. There are no sure investments. Watch the dollar do the dirty float – like a mind, a dead idea, fading out" (55–6). Like any other "investments," all psychological attempts to buy inviolable security are doomed to failure.

Having resolved, on the other hand, to speak for himself, to measure the world through tracking his own movements (in his lecture, Creeley etymologizes "auto-bio-graphy" as "a life tracking itself" [49]), he finds that such self-limitation leads to boundless possibilities for self-exploration. In the broader context of American poetry, Emily Dickinson, a poet to whom Creeley has often been compared, offers a pioneering example of how to follow this autobiographical discipline of measuring the world by tracking one's own movements. Thoreau's self-exploration, like Olson's, is presented in geographical terms; he speaks of being "a Columbus to whole new continents and worlds within you, opening new channels, not of trade, but of thought" (*W*, 212) and offers the "direct way to India": "If you would learn to speak all tongues and conform to the customs of all nations, if you would travel farther than all travellers, be naturalized in all climes, and cause the Sphinx to dash her head against a stone, even obey the precept of the old philosopher, and Explore thyself. Here are demanded the eye and the nerve. Only the defeated and deserters go to the wars, cowards that run away and enlist" (*W*, 213).

Walden is full of meditations upon containment as an instrument for a self-knowledge informed by a particular place and time. Right at the outset, for instance, Thoreau inverts the geographical image of exploration, stating his credentials as a keen observer of human nature by ironically contrasting his book to the best-selling travel narratives of the day: "I have travelled a good deal in Concord" (*W*, 2). This was not only a joke but was quite literally true: Thoreau became, as he counseled in a quote from William Habbington, "Expert in home-cosmography" (*W*, 211). Speaking, alternatively, of the care that Walden Pond itself exercises – preserving what we might call its "self-respect" by keeping its distance from encroaching conformity – he notes how it rises periodically to kill off the vegetation that threatens to take over its banks: "and thus the *shore* is *shorn*" (*W*, 122) and self-containment ensured. And in an even more emphatic rhetorical gesture toward containment, Thoreau conjures up a fanciful etymology for the pond that takes account of the regularity of the rock formations around it: "one might suppose that it was called, originally, *Walled-in* Pond" (*W*, 122).

Advancing this thesis in the most enigmatic and contradictory chapter of *Walden*, "Higher Laws," Thoreau goes so far as to praise chastity for its quality of containment: "The generative energy, which, when we are loose, dissipates and makes us unclean, when we are continent invigorates and inspires us" (*W*, 146). Although there is not a little puritanical guilt mixed in with this uncomfortably Victorian diction, he appears in this chapter to be praising chastity as a means of paying attention, pitting it against the universal entropic tendency toward dullness: "What is chastity? How shall a man know if he is chaste? He shall not know it. We have heard of this virtue, but we know not what it is. . . . From exertion come wisdom and purity; from sloth ignorance and sensuality. In the student sensuality is a sluggish habit of mind" (*W*, 147). Thoreau problematizes the term "chastity," averring that we don't really know what it is; he goes on to hint that beyond sexual abstinence chastity functions as a metaphor for the contained use of energy. Considerably more macho and less squeamish than Thoreau, Olson also ties continence to containment:

> When I look at the filth and lumber which man is led by, I see man's greatest achievement in this childish accomplishment – that he damn well can, and does, destroy destroy destroy energy every day. It is too much. It is too much to waste time on, this idiot who spills his fluids like some truculent and fingerless chamaco hereabouts [in the Yucatán] who wastes water at the pump when birds are dying all over the country in this hottest of the months. . . . (*SW*, 63)[14]

For both Olson and Thoreau, mental incontinence is a cardinal sin, which Olson characterizes as an acquiescence in entropy, through which

human beings can be said to "destroy destroy destroy energy every day."
When Olson rails against "the lumber and filth which man is led by," he
means not only national leaders but, in the context of this passage, scholars who "do not know how to pass over to us the energy implicit in any
high work of the past" (*SW*, 63). The scholar is guilty when he pursues
knowledge as mere accumulation (a form of greed) rather than as a necessary aspect of self-understanding and as a foundation for contained encounter with the present. "It is unbearable what knowledge of the past
has been allowed to become, what function of human memory has drib-
bled out to in the hands of these learned monsters whom people are led to
think 'know' " (*SW*, 63). Thoreau, too, values attention and care (*Max*,
32) over almost any other virtues, to the extent that, in the midst of his
discussion of chastity, America's greatest "nature writer" makes the sur-
prising statement that "Nature is hard to be overcome, but she must be
overcome" (*W*, 147). Even nature is subordinate to mental continence in
Thoreau's hierarchy of values, so that the "unnaturalness" of chastity can,
at least provisionally, be placed above it.

For all his agreement with Thoreau on the virtues of mental continence, Olson does not countenance Thoreau's somewhat morbid distrust
of flesh in "Higher Laws." For Olson, self-containment need not be
insulation from other human beings or from nature; in fact, an unself-
consciousness about the flesh should naturally accompany the outward
gaze of a self-contained individual. In this regard, Olson finds in the
contemporary Maya of the Yucatán two accomplishments that attest to
the former greatness of their civilization: "it is only love and flesh which
seems to carry any sign of their antecedence"; he notices these graces "as
their bodies jostle in a bus, or as they disclose the depth and tenacity of
love among each other inside a family." The Maya, Olson observes,

> do one thing no modern knows the secret of . . . : they wear their
> flesh with that difference which the understanding that it is com-
> mon leads to. When I am rocked by the roads against any of them –
> kids, women, men – their flesh is most gentle, is granted, touch is
> in no sense anything but the natural law of flesh, there is none of
> that pull-away which, in the States, causes a man for all the years of
> his life the deepest sort of questioning of the rights of himself to the
> wild reachings of his own organism. The admission these people
> give me and one another is direct, and the individual who peers out
> from that flesh is precisely himself, is a curious wandering animal
> like me – it is so very beautiful how animal human eyes are when
> the flesh is not worn so close it chokes, how human and individu-
> ated the look comes out of a human eye when the house of it is not
> exaggerated. (*SW*, 57)[15]

Containment, as Olson imagines it, does not foster rigid isolation or defensive self-enclosure; it situates us resolutely in the common, making possible expansive gestures like the dignified yielding of flesh that he senses among the Maya. Although still unwilling to yield (to) the flesh, Thoreau explores the issue of containment with regard to other people and to nature in the twin chapters, "Solitude" and "Visitors," in a less reactive way than he does in "Higher Laws." These chapters are full of provocative insights into the relationship of self-sufficiency to a careful attunement with nature and other human beings, but the most subtle and instructive observation concerns the ultimate goal of self-containment. Speaking of the content of the beautiful gaze that, as Olson says, "comes out of a human eye when the house of it is not exaggerated," Thoreau notes that it arises from a paradoxical doubleness within containment itself:

> With thinking we may be beside ourselves in a sane sense. By a conscious effort of the mind we can stand aloof from actions and their consequences; and all things, good and bad, go by us like a torrent. We are not wholly involved in Nature. I may be either the driftwood in the stream, or Indra in the sky looking down on it. I *may* be affected by a theatrical exhibition; on the other hand, I *may not* be affected by an actual event which appears to concern me much more. I only know myself as a human entity; the scene, so to speak, of thoughts and affections; and am sensible of a certain doubleness by which I stand as remote from myself as from another. However intense my experience, I am conscious of the presence and criticism of a part of me, which, as it were, is not a part of me, but spectator, sharing no experience, but taking note of it; and this is no more I than it is you. When the play, it may be the tragedy, of life is over, the spectator goes his way. It was a kind of fiction, a work of the imagination only, so far as he was concerned. (*W,* 90–1)

When Thoreau says in this passage that "we are not wholly involved in Nature," he is saying something quite different from "Nature is hard to be overcome, but she must be overcome." The separation from nature Thoreau posits here is one not of opposition but of heightened awareness. This awareness comes as a result of carrying through to their fullest extent the spiritual implications of containment. At this extreme, the self seems to split into a double entity, an actor and what Whitman calls a "witness," leaving one "both in and out of the game" (*LG,* 32). Discovery of the witness or "spectator" affords Thoreau the freedom both to give himself fully to a fictional drama (participating in its creative representation without reserve) and to view his own life as merely another drama (distancing himself from an egotistical concern with its outcome). Achieving this perspective, he finds that the anxiety of self-consciousness (manifest, as Olson puts it, in "the deepest sort of questioning of the rights of himself to the wild reachings of his own organism") dissolves; the witness is that self which is "at once center and circumference" (*SVH,* 36), which allows us to see the facts of the present moment from the most expanded perspective.[16]

This sense of doubleness, in which one splits into a witness and an embodied actor, accords exactly with Olson's exhortation to view ourselves as objects: "For a man is himself an object, whatever he may take to be his advantages, the more likely to recognize himself as such the greater his advantages, particularly at that moment that he achieves an humilitas sufficient to make him of use" (*SW,* 24–5). In the dissolution of ego forced by a thoroughgoing containment, the consciousness seems to split free from the body, not in order to desert it but rather to stop "choking" it, thus to direct it in the most energetic and useful ways possible. In recounting his experience of this split, Thoreau speaks the same White-headian language that Olson was to adopt, in which entities are viewed as events in process (rather than as composed of substance and form): "I only know myself as a human entity; the scene, so to speak, of thoughts and affections; and am sensible of a certain doubleness by which I can stand as remote from myself as from another." In order for a poet to become situated in the "field" that Olson calls projective verse, she or he must become capable of containment as a witness.

At the opening of *The Maximus Poems,* Olson presents Maximus as a witness, located both "off-shore" from Gloucester and as a consciousness hidden within the body:

> Off-shore, by islands hidden in the blood
> jewels & miracles, I, Maximus
> a metal hot from boiling water, tell you
> what is a lance, who obeys the figures of
> the present dance   (*Max,* 5)

Maximus is the witness at a white heat of intensity, able, in Thoreau's terms, to "stand as remote from [Olson] as from another," in order to look down like Indra from the highest possible vantage point. But Maximus is not separate from Charles Olson; he is a figure for Olson at his most self-sufficient (and therefore maximally expansive). As Sherman Paul puts it: "Maximus is an aspect of Olson ('I, as Maximus,' he says), the naming of what by means of the poem he would become; Maximus is *homo maximus,* Jung's individuated man, the man who has realized the self, who, having reconciled the opposites of his nature, is whole. . . . The one thing to insist on, as Olson did, is that Maximus is not a persona."[17] The figure of Maximus is born from that split into doubleness that occurs at the point of maximum containment. Far from inventing a persona or a mask, Olson conceives of Maximus as the truest representation of Charles Olson – an image of a poet as the active, focal point (lance) of his attention. Although Maximus declares himself forcefully at the beginning of *The Maximus Poems,* he appears less and less visibly as a discrete figure as the book continues; Olson incorporates the oracular voice of Maximus into his own speaking voice (like the "Me myself," the witness in Whitman's "Song of Myself"), so that by the final volume of *The Maximus Poems* Maximus and Olson seem coextensive: The "human and individuated . . . look [that] comes out of [Olson's] eye when the house of it is not exaggerated" belongs to Maximus. Maximus leads Olson on a search for the greatest extensions of human capability, not on a quest for an individual identity. The split into witness and actor functions as an image of contained self-exploration rather than as a sign of a permanent division. This split clarifies and maximizes the powers available to a human being; it is not intended to erect a "Charles Olson" for our admiration: "It is not I, / even if the life appeared / biographical," Olson claims, "The only interesting thing / is if one can be / an image / of man" (*Max, 473*).

The heightened attention of the witness is like a precisely focused laser beam. In an interview, Robert Creeley recounts an anecdote of meeting a wholly self-contained man – a Mayan, in fact – who embodied such a witnessing alertness. Acknowledging the rarity of an encounter with such a radiantly alert individual, Creeley testifies to the momentous quality of the meeting. Like Thoreau, who observes, "I have never yet met a man who was quite awake. How could I have looked him in the face?" (*W,* 61), Creeley records a sense of embarrassment and self-consciousness when confronted by this self-contained and yet unassuming person. The encounter took place, Creeley explains, when he visited "an old time kind of adventurer" in Southern Mexico, who offered him an introduction:

> "How would you like to meet a Mayan?" I said "Terrific!" He said "Actually the man is a Lacandon Indian. He's the first person ever to come out of his particular situation *ever.* The first human being of that particular cluster ever to go beyond its stated boundaries and to move out of its area of habitation into this world." And I said "That would be an honor indeed if in my American sense it wouldn't bother him. If it wouldn't be an imposition upon him I would be honored to meet such a human being." And so he said "He's in the next room I'll ask him to come out." So momently here was this man another human being standing

there   and   in no sense "primitive"   in the sense that his teeth
were filed   the sometime imagination of the primitive   caveman
just another   extraordinary   human being.   I did   again   the
American thing   of putting out my hand.   And   he looked at it
     and then   and I was very relieved.   (*Laughter*) What was extra
ordinary about this man   was   that   all the senses   were absolutely
 alert   all over the body   in the same way you'd experience the situation
of a   so-called   wild animal   as opposed to a domestic animal.
I mean   the sensory system was absolutely alert   not worried
but he was entirely *there*.   I've never met a human being who was so com
pletely   where he *was*   not that he knew where he was   or was de
termined to stay there   but was absolutely   alive in the moment of
     each instant.   I mean   there was no abstraction in him.   It was
fantastic.   I thought   "You *can* do it."   I mean   you *can* arrive at   a
consciousness that's   present as opposed   to one   that's thinking about
what happened last week   or what is going to happen tomorrow   as
an imposition on   the present instance.   Extraordinarily fresh.
He was healthy   and   as one might expect   his whole sensory nervous
system   was absolutely incredible.[18]

Self-containment as a spiritual discipline reaches its goal in the absolute attention to the demands of the present moment. Thoreau, Olson,
and Creeley all believe that focusing so unequivocally upon the facts
before one yields a state of alertness in which the possibilities for action
are boundless. American poetry, in their understanding of it, works by
cultivating this discipline. Although Creeley ultimately applies his alertness to a different poetic method – that of repetition instead of containment – his anecdote combines senses of strangeness and of confirmation
that are hallmarks of the doubleness of tradition, in which the hidden
power of the spectator or witness speaks out from tradition's muteness.

Chapter 3

RESISTANCE AND POETIC COMMUNITY

"GROUND, WALL, CANNON, TOWER"

As his encounter with the Mayan makes clear, Creeley's fascination with awareness drives him not away from the body but more deeply into its experience, particularly as awareness is contained at the body's surface. Informed by this belief in the body's centrality to awareness, he chooses to open his edition of Olson's *Selected Writings* with an essay called "The Resistance." In this brief statement Olson tries to take stock of the drastic reduction of human reality (call it an extreme foreshortening of tradition) precipitated by such events as Auschwitz and Hiroshima; a consequence of this reduction, Olson claims, is that the only tolerable way to inhabit the present moment is to seek a grounding within the human body:

> Man came here by an intolerable way. When man is reduced to so much fat for soap, superphosphate for soil, fillings and shoes for sale, he has, to begin again, one answer, one point of resistance only to such fragmentation, one organized ground, a ground he comes to by a way the precise contrary of the cross, of spirit in the old sense, in old mouths. It is his own physiology he is forced to arrive at.
>
> . . . In this intricate structure are we based, now more certainly than ever (besieged, overthrown), for its power is bone muscle nerve blood brain   a man, its fragile mortal force its old eternity, resistance. (*SW*, 13–14)

Throughout his writing, Olson makes of resistance a primary political virtue. The "root act" (*SW*, 13) of resistance is containment inside the physical body, within the present occasion – an act that yields a liberating recognition: "This is eternity. This now. This foreshortened span" (*SW*, 13). Radically contracting the aperture of attention, excluding layer after layer of self-imaging and social role-playing, one reaches a resistant minimum comprised of the body in a particular setting. By virtue of this

harrowing reduction, one achieves an unshakeable self-possession; re-
trieved from the realms of fantasy and returned to the physical body and
the present occasion, one senses a freedom, an escape from external
manipulation, which sanctions an instant expansion into communion
with others. The order of events occurs along the narrative lines we have
come to expect: turning away from "the fraud" of imagining oneself as a
"cathedral, draughty tenement of soul" (*SW*, 13–14), one resists all lofty
self-conceptions until only the body, as ground, remains; from this precisely located vantage point, opportunities for effective action in the
world open out. In the essay "Proprioception," for instance, Olson turns
away from fraudulent fantasies about the self by reducing psychology to
a matter of the functions of various parts of the body – locating perception on the surface, the unconscious in the internal organs, and the self-
reflexive consciousness that coordinates the other two in proprioception
("sensibility within the organism by movement of its own tissues") (*AP*,
17). Likewise, in "Projective Verse," he traces poetry back to the ear and
the breath: "that verse will only do in which a poet manages to register
both the acquisitions of his ear *and* the pressures of his breath" (*SW*, 17).

The American attempt to ground action and thought in the body
rather than in social roles extends back at least as far as Whitman. At
several points in "Song of Myself," for instance, Whitman enacts a scrupulous reduction to the resistant body. The most notable instance is in
Section 20:

> Who goes there? hankering, gross, mystical, nude;
> How is it I extract strength from the beef I eat?
> . . . .
> Having pried through the strata, analyzed to a hair, counsel'd with
>   doctors and calculated close,
> I find no sweeter fat than sticks to my own bones.
> . . . .
> I exist as I am, that is enough,
> If no other in the world be aware I sit content,
> And if each and all be aware I sit content.
> . . . .
> My foothold is tenon'd and mortis'd in granite,
> I laugh at what you call dissolution,
> And I know the amplitude of time.   (*LG*, 47–48)

Like Olson, Whitman reinstates the body to a central position, acknowledging and honoring it, while resisting other valuations that subordinate
the body to their own categorical manipulations. Through this return to

the body, Whitman reaches bottom in a striking image of corporeal groundedness: "My foothold is tenon'd and mortis'd in granite." "Sitting content" within that imperturbable self-possession, he glimpses his bottomlessness, which allows him, in turn, to refer to himself in the terms employed by the God of the Hebrew Bible: "I exist as I am."

By taking up residence in the resistant body, these poets also acquire an impressive moral force; the power of the body as expressed in adamant self-possession gives one a "firm foundation" from which to address the world and to act. Claiming that moral authority finds grounding in the body rather than in the fantasies of individual aggrandizement we call "the soul," Olson states: "This organism now our citadel never was cathedral, draughty tenement of soul, was what it is: ground, wall, cannon, tower" (SW, 13–14).[1] In a similar vein, Thoreau notes how the bodily self-possession of the American Indians granted them an astonishing moral superiority over their Jesuit torturers: "The Jesuits were quite balked by those Indians who, being burned at the stake, suggested new modes of torture to their tormentors. Being superior to physical suffering, it sometimes chanced that they were superior to any consolation which the missionaries could offer . . ." (W, 50). As political resistors the world over have shown during this century, the most radical and expansive political gesture has become the pitting of the human body against totalitarianism. Confirming the centrality of bodily resistance in Olson's work, poet and critic Don Byrd carefully sets Olson's writing within the context of that struggle:

> Olson is perhaps the first writer to produce a major body of work in full consciousness of the implications of modern totalitarianism. He does not address a situation in which one has choices between this ideology and that one. The contenders in the political struggle are not ideas. Totalitarianism is the organization of perplexed masses who respond to manipulation of their economic vulnerability, their personal confusion, and their spiritual insecurity. Life is organized in the state by accident or whim. Reality itself is called into question; thus the grounds on which ideas might be tested become themselves unreliable. Only by *doing something* does one begin to feel the way concretely through the forms which were so long matters of debate and have been in modern times wholly occluded.[2]

In the face of the modern experience of groundlessness, Olson and Thoreau propose resistant containment as a way of restoring effective power to individuals and to local communities. The main purpose of Thoreau's long "Economy" chapter, for instance, is to demonstrate how the contained individual can triumph over the politics, the economics, and the technology of the day. By taking power into his own hands, Thoreau hoped to provide an object lesson for the citizens of Concord, making it apparent that one need not accept the intolerable suppositions of modern life. Claiming, "I do not propose to write an ode to dejection, but to brag as lustily as chanticleer in the morning, standing on his roost, if only to wake my neighbors up" (*W*, 1), Thoreau directs us to see his experiment in self-containment not as a melancholy retreat from an uncaring world but as a political action with a salutary practical value for his neighbors. These "neighbors," as Stanley Cavell points out, are the people with whom Thoreau can enter a paradoxical political relationship: "Like the *Leviathan*, and the *Second Treatise of Government*, and the *Discourse on the Origin of Inequality* . . . *Walden* is, among other things, a tract of political education, education for membership in the polis. It locates authority in the citizens and it identifies citizens – those with whom one is in membership – as 'neighbors.' What it shows is that education for citizenship is education for isolation [that is, self-containment]" (*Senses*, 85–6). As Thoreau built his "roost" on the shores of Walden, so Olson took up his "nest" on the shores of Cape Ann. Olson's work illustrates an ideal that he considered the basis of the American experiment: he wished to demonstrate how a single human being, investigating the history of his own community in tandem with exploring the wellsprings of his own interior life (as mirrored in the worldwide images of human capability Olson sought out), could reach significantly greater levels of knowledge, coherence, and power than individuals are thought capable of in this time of fragmentation, specialization, professionalism, consumerism, bureaucracy, and so on. As a record of this investigation, *The Maximus Poems*, even more than *Walden*, are proposed as "a tract of political education, education for membership in the polis."

* * * *

Ezra Pound provided the primary example for Olson of a poet seeking personal power in the face of modern institutionalism. Recognizing Pound's authority, Olson often addresses him as the "master," although his relationship to Pound was resoundingly oedipal rather than reverential. The most remarkable document of this relationship is Olson's own record, *Charles Olson & Ezra Pound: An Encounter at St. Elizabeth's*, edited by Catherine Seelye. Through this intimate association with Pound, Olson came to a decisive understanding of the dangerous and quixotic quest for personal power the former had undertaken. In his anxiety over the lack of a coherent tradition in America, Pound played a desperate game of "King of the Mountain," trying to climb to the top of the heap of Western culture with the Faustian goal of arrogating its power and authority to himself. As Olson sees it, Pound's egotism became the basis for his "solution" to the American problem of tradition; rather than, as Eliot did, "altering the existing order of monuments" to make a place for his own work, Pound subsumed those monuments directly into *The Cantos*: "Ez's epic solves problem by his ego: his single emotion breaks all down to his equals or inferiors (so far as I can see only two, possibly, are admitted, by him, to be his betters – Confucius, & Dante" (*SW*, 81–2). Olson views Pound's egotistical struggle to be King of the Mountain as a misguided, disastrous attempt to find a way out of the stifling political structure of contemporary life. Countering this method of self-aggrandizement, Olson tries to reconstitute a posthumanist image of the human large enough to contain all possible powers but ready to fit the shape of any self-contained individual. Pound endeavors to wrap up Western culture as a gift to be passed on magnanimously by the Great Man to his heirs: by not acknowledging the anxiety and egotism that fuel this noble endeavor, Pound becomes a tragic hero rather than a cultural benefactor. Pursuing a discipline of resistant self-containment, Olson hopes to provide a contrary example of the means by which an individual, and by extension a community, could resume possession of maximum powers.

Olson does agree, though, with the Pound of the vorticist years in believing that a handful of individuals could change the world. Robert von Hallberg points out that Olson's faith in his small community at Black Mountain College mirrors his faith in early Gloucester: these are twin images of resistant, self-contained political units. Although because of a community's isolation its breakthroughs may not initially receive adequate attention, such acts of self-containment can have, Olson felt, a decisive effect. In presenting the case of early Gloucester, Olson remarks on

> how small the news was
> a permanent change had come
> by 14 men setting down
> on Cape Ann, on the westerly side
> of the harbor   (*Max*, 124)[3]

From Olson's perspective, the small fishing village in Massachusetts and the artists' community in North Carolina shared a historic commitment: to resist the authority of the state (in the form of the Plymouth Company, in the case of Gloucester, and of administrative bureaucracy, in the case of the self-governing faculty of Black Mountain College) and to create a polis on their own terms and for their own well-being. In both situations, the spirit of resistance provoked what was at the time a virtually unheralded and temporary grounding that has proven capable of endless ramifications. Such resistant self-grounding, exemplified in the struggle of the Gloucester fishermen to combat the usurpation of their fishing station by the Pilgrims, becomes for Olson the foundation of political virtue:

> They should raise a monument
> to a fisherman crouched down
> behind a hogshead, protecting
> his dried fish   (*Max*, 118)

What we have in this field in these scraps among these fishermen, and the Plymouth men, is more than the fight of one colony with another; it is the whole engagement against (1) mercantilism . . . ; and (2) against nascent capitalism except as it stays the individual adventurer and the worker on share – against all sliding statism, ownership getting in to, the community as, Chamber of Commerce, or theocracy; or City Manager (*Max*, 105)

The resistant acts of the self-reliant individual or community produce the truly valuable events of history. In this regard, Olson's central maxim of self-containment, "That which exists through itself is what is called meaning" – with which he begins his "Causal Mythology" lecture (*Muth* I, 64) – describes not only ontology but history. When a Gloucester fisherman saves his dried fish from the hands of the Pilgrim authorities, he does much more, Olson claims, than what classical economists think of as obeying the laws of self-interest. Certainly his "interest" is at stake, but what Olson defines as interest is the value arising from the fisherman's own work and from his attempt to maintain control over the fruits, the conditions, and the meaning of that work. The determined resistance of "14 men setting down / on Cape Ann" provides an accurate measure of the possibilities of an American relationship to work, materials, landscape, and community; Olson points out how aggressively the protestant work ethic has countered such possibilities. As a place for grounding, the American landscape must be approached, he feels, through self-containment rather than rapacity, for only self-containment allows us to "set down" upon, to inhabit carefully, the land.

"TO FIND THE SECRET OF IT"

One reason why Olson wishes to commemorate the early fishermen of Gloucester as "founding fathers" of America – to tell a story which figures them as heroes and the Pilgrims as villains – is because the fishermen respected their own limits, rather than insisting, as so many others have done throughout American history, upon an old, discredited vision of a "new world." Stanley Cavell attributes to Thoreau a similar interpretation of the American condition. Cavell contends that *Walden* was written at a time when "there is an unprecedented din of prophecy," and that therefore Thoreau became an antiprophet, promoting a new interpretation of the prophetic hearsay:

> Everyone is saying, and anyone can hear, that this is the new world, that we are the new men; that the earth is to be born again; that the past is to be cast off like a skin; that we must learn from children to see again; that every day is the first day of the world; that America is Eden. So how can a word get through whose burden is that we do not understand a word of all this? Or rather, that the way in which we understand it is insane, and we are trying again to buy and bully our way into heaven; that we have failed; that the present is a task and a discovery, not a period of America's privileged history; that we are not free, not whole, not new, and we know this and are on a downward path of despair because of it; and that for the child to grow he requires family and familiarity, but for a grownup to grow he requires strangeness and transformation, i.e., birth? (*Senses*, 59–60)

Olson shares Cavell's perception that Americans are so deafened by millennial promises, offered anew in the twentieth century by advertising and public relations, that we have lost the ability to attend to our present situation, which, strange and unimaginable as it is, offers our only true hope of redemption. In his own day, Olson finds that the "din of prophecy" echoing down from Puritan times has become, if anything, much louder; it speaks through all of the media that intrude into virtually every public and private moment of our lives:

> But that which matters, that which insists, that which will last, that! o my people, where shall you find it, how, where, where shall you listen
> when all is become billboards, when, all, even silence, is spray-gunned?
> . . . .
> when even you, when sound itself is neoned in? (*Max*, 6)

Only the rare, resistant individual, "if he stays inside himself, if he is contained within his nature" (*SW*, 25), can become a model and a measure for that even rarer entity, the resistant community. The true worker, whether a fisherman or a poet, turns aside from the sticky stream of prophecy sprayed through the public communications media and bends instead to the work at hand.

Like fishermen, poets too have "crouched down / behind a hogshead, protecting" their work from appropriation, resisting valiantly the prophetic cries of critics who too easily discover in the poetry a manipulable "truth" that was already ringing in their own ears. Olson's poems, and those of the projectivists with whom he was associated, put up a staunch resistance to reductive interpretation. The poems refuse to passively yield their "dried fish," insisting instead upon remaining peculiarly self-sufficient. Echoing the principle of self-sufficiency that he discovered in the Taoist text, *The Secret of the Golden Flower*[4] – "That which exists through itself is what is called meaning" – Olson speaks of his poems as issuing into an unforeseen, uncontrollable present, like plums from flowering fruit trees:

> until one discovers
> there is no other issue than
> the moment of
>   the pleasure of
>   this plum,
>
> these things
> which don't carry their end any further than
> their reality in
> themselves   (*Max,* 46)

According to the objectivist poetics to which Olson subscribes, a poem is a self-contained object, resisting appropriation into terms other than its own; its meaning takes place in its own self-unfoldment, in its cleaving to itself. The poems retain a mysterious fecundity through refusing easy entry.

Many a reader has felt that if a poem proves that resistant to approach, then maybe one had better leave it alone. Isn't it just a matter, one wonders, of a secret that the poet (accompanied, perhaps, by a select cohort) is hiding – a secret the knowledge of which would render this obfuscated text transparent but which the reader is barred from discerning? Olson would probably acknowledge the existence of a secret while maintaining that knowing it will not suddenly make a poem transparent. The secret can and should be known (the bottom), but knowing it does not dissolve the poem's mystery (its bottomlessness). Rather than the key to a code, which might allow us to decipher something formerly unintelligible, the secret is an attitude toward life, a way of participating bodily in it. In his essay on D. H. Lawrence's *Man Who Died,* "The Escaped Cock: Notes on Lawrence & the Real," Olson identifies the central question that Lawrence raises for Jesus as: "Is anything worth more than the most precise sharpening of the instrument, a human, to the hearing of – the hearing of *all* there is *in* – the bronze clang of a cock's crow? / (Is an X-fiction worth a cock's crow?)" (*HU,* 124). Saying no to the first question and yes to the second, Olson remarks that, "such hearing (to find the secret of it, which means, of course, to recognize it, then to admit it, then, of all, to participate) is worth the coming back, the putting behind one, the over-looking a Crucifixtion [*sic*]" (*HU,* 125). There is a secret in the cock's crow, which is found not just by "hearing" it but also by "recognizing" it, then by "admitting" it, and finally by "participating" in it. Olson identifies the secret as an attitude toward life that involves an alert recognition of it, an admission of its value, and a direct participation in it. If the Crucifixion is a sacrifice of life that redeems it only outside itself, then Olson's secret runs in the counterdirection – into full participation.

Possession of a secret would seem to separate the writer from the common way, but then, paradoxically, the secret turns out to be an injunction to participation (keeping one "both in and out of the game" [*LG,* 32] – as Whitman says, extolling the witness that arises from self-containment). Reporting the frustration of his initial attempts to try to understand Olson, Don Byrd notes how in sensing the secret concealed in the work, the reader feels like a cautious outsider: "I felt at times that I was falling prey to a cult leader, a man who was insidiously subverting my knowledge in order to replace it with a mystery of his own. I suspect that it is this feeling which makes some readers resist Olson's work."[5] This feeling of discomfort does conceal a truth: the Black Mountain poets functioned as a kind of mystery sect, particularly between the years of 1950, when Olson and Creeley began corresponding and Cid Corman started *Origin,* and 1970, when Olson died. As the leader, Olson encouraged a host of others to join this community of resistant poets. Thus, a group of writers formed around such centers as Black Mountain College, *Origin,* and *The Black Mountain Review*: Olson, Creeley, Duncan, Corman, Denise Levertov, Edward Dorn, Paul Blackburn, Joel Oppenheimer, Fielding Dawson, Michael Rumaker, Hilda Morley, John Wieners, Larry Eigner, Jonathan Williams, Le Roi Jones, Gilbert Sorrentino, and others. In the course of this twenty-year period, a second wave of projectivist writers appeared and intermingled with the first; of a larger number that could be mentioned, the following writers maintained a more or less strict adherence to the projectivist doctrine during at least some of this time: Robert Kelly, Theodore Enslin, Kenneth Irby, Jerome Rothenberg, Clayton Eshleman, Edward Sanders, David Bromige, Richard Grossinger, Ronald Johnson, and Armand Schwerner.

Although the projectivist doctrine cannot be reduced merely to the poetics of Charles Olson, his writings (in particular, his essays) did provide a rallying point for the community. Instead of taking credit for inventing the "secret" that these poets share, Olson "finds" a number of formulations of it in his reading and in his dreams: "What does not change / is the will to change" (Plutarch/Heraclitus); "That which exists through itself is what is called meaning" (Lu Tzu); "Life *is* preoccupation with itself" (dream); "Man is estranged from that with which he is most familiar" (Heraclitus); "Form is nothing more than an extension of content" (Creeley); and so on. Olson regards both the possession of a secret and an attitude toward it not of defensiveness but of containment as critical for forming and maintaining a center around which the thoughts and actions of both an individual and a community constellate.

In "The Praises," he investigates an earlier sect, the Pythagoreans, in order to understand the importance of secrecy; it was, he finds, a matter of life and death:

> Says   Iamblichus:
> by shipwreck, he perished (Hippasus, that is)
> the first to publish (write down, divulge)
> the secret,
> the construction of, from 12 pentagons,
> the sphere
>
> "Thus was he punished for his impiety"
> (*CP*, 100)

Since the Enlightenment, we have lost generally that sense of outrage at the divulgence of a secret. In fact, in the wake of demonic examples such as Hitler, the Manson cult, Jonestown, and Islamic fundamentalism, we are more likely to be frightened by the existence of a cult than concerned about the preservation of a special knowledge. Olson proposes, not a cult of believers, but a community of poets and scholars dedicated to an active use of knowledge. From this perspective, he laments the contemporary worship of information as a forfeiting of the benefits of secrecy; we no longer understand the value of social containment for focusing personal power.

> What has been lost
> is the secret of secrecy, is
> the value, viz., that the work get down, and quickly,
> without the loss of due and profound respect for
> the materials
>
> which is not so easy as it sounds, nor
> can it permit the dispersion which follows from
> too many having too little
> knowledge   (*CP*, 100)

The value of the secret does not reside in the particular items of knowledge – for instance, how to construct a sphere from twelve pentagons – but rather how that knowledge is used. Knowledge is ubiquitous, especially in the Age of Information, but because we don't know how to use it, it will always be, Olson judges, "too little." A secret worth knowing is a lodestone or focusing device, which must be contained, meditated upon at length, and applied to all aspects of life, so that it becomes a controlling principle for organizing experience and understanding. The secret functions like a *yantra*, a Tantric design for meditation, which is a map at once individual, social, and cosmic. The secret has an efficacious power directly proportionate to the degree to which we put it to work in the diverse spheres of life. It must be used. And to remain viable it must be transmitted directly from one "container" to another:

What is necessary is
containment,
that that which has been found out by work, may, by work, be
    passed on
(without due loss of force)
for use
    USE   (*CP*, 100)

Olson believes that the formulations of the secret he has discovered in dreams and in various texts can function as effective organizing principles for an active life, whether as a poet, a fisherman, or a waitress.[6] Although the secret is not hidden – he proclaims it vociferously in his writing – it remains mysterious: "what is related must remain enigmatic" (*CP*, 99). Usually, one does not become an initiate except, as they say in Zen Buddhism, "by direct transmission." The contagious excitement, the sometimes bumptious partisan commitment, the seductive sense of certainty about mysterious matters that one finds in the initiate: these qualities, either singly or in combination, have proven fascinating or repellent to observers of the Black Mountain group. When Olson describes the workings of a poem in "Projective Verse" as "energy transferred from where the poet got it . . . , by way of the poem itself to, all the way over to, the reader" and demands that it "must, at all points, be a high energy-construct and, at all points, an energy-discharge" (*SW*, 16), he is also describing the social dynamics of projectivism, directing how its initial impetus and formulation will be transferred to a wide circle of adherents. Through the intensity of their association over the twenty-year period 1950–70, four poets – Olson, Creeley, Levertov, and Duncan – were primarily responsible for generating a kind of energy dynamo, the force of which still continues to be transferred from individual to individual, as the process of initiation repeats itself.

"I TAKE IT WISDOM, LIKE STYLE,
IS THE MAN"

It is easy to see why this esoteric aspect of projectivist poetry has been misunderstood or has proven offensive to people who have not met or have not been particularly captivated by an individual adherent. An allegiance to the projectivist principles is no guarantee of good poetry or of good living. The most beneficent function of these principles, as Olson insisted at every opportunity, is to foster the sense of self-containment that will gradually render a person more and more alive and active. The goal is to "stand more / revealed" (*Max*, 9), to recognize "This very thing you are" (*SW*, 171). There is no need, for example, to subscribe to particular expressions of value – such as Olson's pontifications regarding the worth of one or another writer – or to approve of the alternately bullying and plaintive sides of his character, in order to make full use of the secret he offers. In the projectivist community, all power resides in the active, engaged, self-contained individual: "If there is any absolute, it is never more than this one, you, this instant, in action" (*SW*, 55). In his open letter to Robert Duncan, "Against Wisdom as Such" (published in the first issue of *The Black Mountain Review* [1954]), Olson counterposes his sense of the paramount importance of individual responsibility to what he sees as sectarian abuses of secrecy, whether among poets or in other sects:

> I take it wisdom, like style, is the man – that it is not extricable in any sort of a statement of itself; even though – and here is the catch – there be "wisdom," that it must be sought, and that "truths" can be come on. . . . But they are, in no wise, or at the gravest loss, verbally separated. They stay the man. As his skin is. As his life. And to be parted with only as that is.
> Only sectaries can deal with wisdom as separable. And even they do it by symbols and by signs, and in secret. . . . And I think two things: (1) that such secrecy is wearing the skin that truth is inside-out; and (2) that, as Duncan has so finely made Confucius say, the third of the civilized pleasures cannot ever be conspiracy simply that it is "Perspective" – which is everywhere and every thing, when it is "contained."
> "Contained." I fall back on a difference I am certain the poet at least has to be fierce about: that he is not free to be a part of, or to be any, sect; that there are no symbols to him, there are only his own composed forms, and each one solely the issue of the time of the moment of its creation, not any ultimate except what he in his heat and that instant in its solidity yield. (*HU*, 68–9)

As Olson characterizes it, the false sect deals in occult symbols, which can be separated from the actual experiences of its members and used for political power; likewise, the sect hides its secrets in a conspiratorial silence ("inside-out"), demanding allegiance to its absolute "wisdom." Writing during the McCarthy era, Olson made it clear that his own notion of the poetic community operated in direct opposition to authoritarian conspiracies; a poetic community must be governed by the containment that supports individual initiative. Referring to the paranoid climate of the times ("as I sit in the midst of these dreary States, all atomic and anti-Russian events served up to people to kill them off with botulism before botulism" [HU, 67–8]), Olson says, of wisdom, "The subject is a matter of importance, now that the wisdom of the East and the unwisdom of the West are both being looked to as dispensations, by the Right and the right Right" (HU, 69). The example of the self-contained individual must be forcefully raised, as it was in the great mystery religions of the past, to counter the paranoid sectarianism of the present. Fidelity to one's own experience and circumstances fosters a largeness of heart, which Olson pictures as "the third of the civilized pleasures. . . . 'Perspective' – which is everywhere and every thing, when it is 'contained.' "

By submitting to the discipline of containment, a writer's perspective is not narrowed and rigidified but rather expanded and intensified. Thoreau likewise endorses a self-contained wisdom that counters narrow sectarianism, vowing that

> with wisdom we shall learn liberality. The solitary hired man on a farm in the outskirts of Concord, who has had his second birth and peculiar religious experience, and is driven as he believes into silent gravity and exclusiveness by his faith, may think it is not true; but Zoroaster, thousands of years ago, travelled the same road and had the same experience; but he, being wise, knew it to be universal, and treated his neighbors accordingly, and is even said to have invented and established worship among men. (W, 73)

From the examples of ancient cults such as the Zoroastrians, the Pythagoreans, and the Sufis, Thoreau and Olson find models of the preservation and the social utility of "wisdom" passed on from one initiate to another through poetic or spiritual practices. As Olson keeps insisting, though, wisdom is ultimately not a matter of belonging to a particular sect; it is a matter of recognizing the mode of living proper to each unique human being.

In *The Heart of Philosophy*, a book that shares some of the spirit and many of the goals of Olson's attempt to revive an ancient mystery religion in the modern world, Jacob Needleman explores the impact of the

Pythagorean cult upon ancient philosophy and the deleterious effects of its demise. Like Olson, Needleman insists that "This question of the transmission of ideas is absolutely central . . . the neglect of this issue is a principal cause of the fact that reasoning and knowledge themselves have lost their moral power in our lives."[7] With the disappearance of the social background of a community of knowers, dedicated to transmitting particular principles, a major philosophical distinction is lost. Needleman characterizes this distinction as between two types of knowledge, "ideas" and "concepts":

> The first type may be regarded as a sort of energy, a higher energy that can, under very exact conditions, enter into the life of man with transforming effect. . . . The verbal formulation of these ideas is only one aspect, though of course an important aspect, of the conditions necessary for the transmission of the energy they contain. The other conditions are many and varied, including certain forms of communal relations and the employment of many different kinds of symbolic methods – art, architecture, music, dance; as well as a certain orientation toward the needs of the body with respect to diet, sex, sleep, physical work, vocation, and numerous other factors. Here the verbal, conceptual formulation of ideas is only one element in a remarkable sort of overall existential training in which a greater energy is assimilated in the developing human being. (Needleman, 45)

This first type of knowledge, "ideas," corresponds to the "secret" Olson wishes to contain, whose ramifications are roughly those outlined by Needleman. Although he never went to far as to prescribe a particular regimen for the body, Olson sought – at Black Mountain College, in particular – settings where all cultural activities, such as art, architecture, music, and dance, would reinforce the secret. The second type of knowledge, "concepts," comprises the utilitarian tools of thought that Westerners have used to achieve political and scientific dominance over the world. Although neither writer advocates a wholesale abandonment of concepts, both contend that a proper discrimination between ideas and concepts will restore priority to "secrets" and thus help return us to responsible action.

Going beyond the Pythagorean lineage offered by Plutarch, Needleman considers at some length the possible transmission of ideas from Pythagoras to Socrates and thus on to Plato. The crucial question, Needleman argues, in trying to uncover this chain of transmission would be,

> What is the teaching behind the Socratic silence, the Socratic power of self-interrogation? There must have been ideas about man and the

universe behind this power – ideas far, far beyond the quality of mere
theories, concepts, and explanations. The Socratic silence is higher
than "knowledge." . . . But there must have been behind this silence, this "ignorance," a knowledge-not-in-quotation-marks.
(Needleman, 42)

This quotation-mark-free knowledge that exists in silence corresponds to
the notion of tradition as a giving that withholds. Such an uncontrollable
knowledge would have to be embodied in the energy of the teacher, that
"heat," as Olson calls it, that he or she must transmit. This "embodiment
of knowledge" (the title of William Carlos Williams's volume on the
organic process of education), in which silence often acts as a most
powerful teaching, is what the community seeks to preserve in its initiates
and what the loss of containment disperses into mere concepts. The
community fosters the embodiment and transmission of knowledge by
using an idea as a directive center for all the multifarious activities of a
life. When this discipline is fully carried through, one becomes one's secrets; as Olson puts it, " 'truths' can be come on," but they are not be to
"verbally separated. They stay the man. As his skin is. As his life. And to
be parted with only as that is" (*HU*, 68). Comparing ideas to skin, Olson
emphasizes not only how corporeal and sensitive they are but also how
crucial they are to life; their successful investiture is a matter of life and
death.

Ideas are active in a more fundamental way than concepts are: once
clearly formulated, concepts are easy to communicate and relatively easy
to combine for analytical purposes; ideas, however, can provide and even
transform the attitudes we take toward concepts. Ideas can also stop the
incessant flow of concepts in our thoughts in order to effect a complete
internal reorientation. "The authentic formulation of great ideas has the
effect of bringing a man to silence, of stopping the mind. That is to say,
the formulations of great ideas can create in us the state of self-
questioning" (Needleman, 46). Without authentic ideas to guide one,
self-containment is difficult:

The point is obvious to anyone who has attempted serious self-
observation. Without real ideas to guide the attention from within,
the study of oneself soon reaches an insurmountable barrier created
in part by the thoughts and concepts that are conditioned into the
mind by the surrounding culture or subculture. Ideas are necessary
in order to become free from concepts. Incarnated in a great teacher, great ideas become pure energy and love – the teacher acts and
lives the ideas; they are his being. The teacher is his knowledge.
(Needleman, 42)

"EVERYTHING ISSUES FROM THE BLACK CHRYSANTHEMUM"

Let us explore one of Olson's frequently stated secrets, in order to see how he arrives at and employs an idea. For his lecture, "Causal Mythology," delivered at the Berkeley Poetry Conference on July 20, 1965, he proposed as an epigraph one of his principles: *"that which exists through itself is what is called meaning"* (*Muth* I, 64). George Butterick notes that this statement forms "the opening passage of the Chinese sacred text translated by Richard Wilhelm as *The Secret of the Golden Flower* (London, 1945), p. 23: 'Master Lu Tzu said: That which exists through itself is called Meaning (*Tao*). Meaning has neither name nor force. It is the one essence, the one primordial spirit' " (*Muth* I, 208). In a note to an essay of Olson's entitled "Experience and Measurement" (posthumously published in *Olson* 3 [1975]), Butterick reproduces Olson's marginalia on the opening passage of *The Secret of the Golden Flower* quoted above: "I am / that I am / The Great *One* is that which exists through itself; nothing is above it because it is contained in the Light of Heaven" (63). To make the context of Olson's response a bit clearer, here is the same passage from a revised version of the text:

> Master Lü-tsu said, That which exists through itself is called the Way (Tao). Tao has neither name nor shape. It is the one essence, the one primal spirit. Essence and life cannot be seen. They are contained in the light of heaven. The light of heaven cannot be seen. It is contained in the two eyes. To-day I will be your guide and will first reveal to you the secret of the Golden Flower of the great One, and, starting from that, I will explain the rest in detail.
>
> The great One is the term given to that which has nothing above it. The secret of the magic of life consists in using action in order to attain non-action. One must not wish to leap over everything and penetrate directly. The maxim handed down to us is to take in hand the work on human nature (*hsing*). In doing this it is important not to take any wrong path.
>
> The Golden Flower is the light. What color is the light? One uses the Golden Flower as a symbol. It is the true energy of the transcendent great One.[8]

The Taoist text seems to proceed by a series of equivalences, which Olson in turn takes up in his marginal note. The Golden Flower is a symbol of the light of heaven, which is a spiritual principle (it cannot be seen; rather, it is the consciousness that sees, which is "contained" in sight); the light of heaven is an expression of the nameless, formless Tao; the Tao is the self-existent. Olson juxtaposes these equations of the Tao with God's name, "I am that I am" (which had also, as we have seen, fascinated Whitman), in order to equate God with this Taoist principle of radiant self-existence. By suppressing the word *Tao* in his formulation, "that which exists through itself is what is called meaning," Olson deflects attention away from the "exotic" quality of Taoism (in "Against Wisdom as Such" he complains about the sectarian uses of the *I Ching*) and from theological terms in general and concentrates instead on an interpretation of "meaning" as produced through the self-grounding existence of an object rather than through the manipulation of concepts. In his essay "Human Universe," Olson specifically contrasts the meaningfulness of self-existence to conceptually constructed meaning as it is achieved through comparison:

> we do not find ways to hew to experience as it is, in our definition and expression of it, in other words, find ways to stay in the human universe, and not be led to partition reality at any point, in any way. . . . It is the function, *comparison,* or, its bigger name, *symbology.* These are the false faces, too much seen, which hide and keep from us the active intellectual states, metaphor and performance. All that comparison ever does is set up a series of reference points: to compare is to take one thing and try to understand it by marking its similarities to or differences from another thing. Right here is the trouble, that each thing is not so much like or different from another thing (these likenesses and differences are apparent) but that such an analysis only accomplishes a *description,* does not come to grips with what really matters: that a thing, any thing, impinges on us by a more important fact, its self-existence, without reference to any other thing, in short, the very character of it which calls our attention to it, which wants us to know more about it, its particularity. (*SW,* 56)

Highly sensitized as we are to the creation of meaning through a play of differences, we may question what kind of meaning there can be without comparison, description, classification. For instance, if all things have meaning only in and of themselves, then what possible relationship can a human being have toward them? Or if, on the other hand, one adopts an extreme nominalist position, insisting that abstract terms have no reality, then what sort of measure can one apply to the world and to human actions? Olson attempted to answer these questions for himself in a sometimes maddeningly obscure manuscript, dated "Wednesday night March 16th/1966," which he called "Experience and Measurement." In this handwritten essay he refers to a dream from early 1958, in which he was given the secret, "Everything issues from the Black Chrysanthemum, and nothing is anything but itself measured so" (*Olson* 3:59).[9] The

Black Chrysanthemum is a variation upon the Golden Flower (*chrys-an-themum* means "gold flower"), and, as Olson notes in his essay, this "message" bears a close family resemblance to Lü-tsu's opening statement. If we take the Taoist pronouncement together with Olson's, "then we do have, in these two statements, the total argument at least of existence as tied at once to both measurement and 'the Meaning' " (ibid.). Olson reasons that because everything issues from one entity, the Black Chrysanthemum (or the Tao), everything is both related and meaningful. To come into existence is to enter a relatedness of being, which all entities share, but which cannot be reduced to conceptual terms: "Measurement is this fact – that everything does issue from the Black Chrysanthemum & *therefore* nothing is anything but itself" (60).[10] If the ground of being is the Tao rather than the Logos of Western philosophy, then this sort of ground is equivalent to the double-natured tradition, which both gives us the names from the past and refuses us any grounds for comparison that would grant us a sense of safety or control. Within each name, as within each thing, resides the bottomless power that makes it meaningful: to recognize meaning, we should not seek to compare things to one another but rather to penetrate deeply enough into each thing that we find the unending Tao within it.

Olson goes on to claim that there is an important human corollary to this cosmic principle of the consanguinity of all things as issues of the Black Chrysanthemum: the human necessity is to *recognize* this fact to the maximum degree, so that one's life becomes fully endowed with meaning. Olson had a startling recognition of the cosmic measurement of meaning when he ingested psilocybin mushrooms: "My own experience, under the mushroom for the first time, was literally tak[ing] a bite straight out of the creation, I couldn't believe what I heard, that everybody said – as though they were coming, in anything they said or did, straight from the creation, straight from truth itself" (61). Olson understood his psychedelic experience as a vision of the extraordinary meaningfulness of every event; to have this vision is to participate in self-measure as meaning:

> That then is the double: that we, in short, because we are, because we do issue from this Named Thing we have the Meaning only to the degree that we transfer this fact – this measure, that we like everything else are only anything because everything is itself only – to ourselves successfully enough that we only exist through a[n] identical condition, the condition herein called & knowable as *through itself*, as actively become ourselves itself as all is anyway, direct from the Black Gold flower. (61)

Confessing that he has "spelled this out – & spilled purposely what is known as the 'Secret,' " Olson finds it necessary to disavow any sectarian motives. Rather than wishing to capitalize as an "adept" (61) upon his discovery of this truth, he hopes to make it available to anyone capable of receiving it. At the end of the essay, he takes one last stab at stating the principle, this time in a language that seems deliberately philosophical: "nothing is anything but itself measured by the fact that everything issues from one Named & Known or knowable fact and that there is no other Meaning than that which exists through itself has become or can then be the Meaning" (62). The only thing meaningful is creation, and all creation is self-creation.

Two years later, in the lecture "Poetry and Truth," delivered in March of 1968, Olson presented these ideas to an audience. The secret discussed in "Experience and Measurement" represents Olson's "Truth," which he felt ambivalent about revealing – not because he wanted to hide the truth but because he feared it would be misinterpreted. Olson had an avid interest in occult matters like alchemy, Sufism, the Tarot, and Jungian psychology, but he scrupulously distanced himself from the sectarian attitudes many people adopt when studying such subjects. During the lecture, Olson hinted to the audience, "You can hear how many things I'm avoiding, no? in order to talk of this subject. I think it's quite obvious that the thing here is to be clear without referring to all that has previously been brought to bear on this word. I mean truth" (*Muth* II, 48). Not only does he wish to avoid all of the occult, theological, and philosophical formulations of truth, he doesn't even want to name his own sources or make the background of his own idea too specific:

> It's Chinese, and so that your minds will not be teased, or so that your minds may learn not to be teased, don't be teased that I don't use its title. This, I'm sure, is not practiced, but again my masters hold their hands upon their lips. . . .

> "That which exists through itself, is what is called meaning." Too much! I mean it's too much for me to stand here and just have that. And that *is* what I have to offer. And that's what I think there is to offer, and I don't think anything in this world moves it a jot, except as we do, or become such. "That which exists through itself is what is called meaning." And even that word *meaning* is, I think, very – I'm reading from a translation of the Chinese, and . . . the word, of course, in Chinese is that word which I would like to avoid mentioning, but it rhymes with the man who also, to whom it is attributed. And we have that word in our language as "how," if you get my string of rhymes.

I – and again, if you'll excuse me – I will keep my noun. I once was told this, by myself, to myself, by no body or thing that I could identify. I think I was asleep, and it was a dream. But what got said was, "Everything issues from – Everything issues from . . . [Olson's ellipsis], and nothing is anything but itself, measured so." Which I'm sure led me on the path to the door of this sentence ["That which exists . . . "], quite simply. Can you hear? May I, would you like me to just repeat that? It's easy. I mean, it's like a prayer. Not really – a bead, something I carry in my pocket. I've never said this out loud, that's how much I love youse here now. Nobody ever heard me say this before. And still I have something for myself – by even telling you that much. "Everything issues from . . . , and nothing is anything but itself, measured so." (*Muth* II, 48–51)

The Secret of the Black Chrysanthemum operated as an idea for Olson in Needleman's sense of a higher teaching informing the life and work at every level. In *The Maximus Poems,* for example, the Black Chrysanthemum becomes a central image, associated with the ocean (2, 172–6, 180), with Heraclitus (172), with Whitehead (501–2), with the sun (181, 441), with heaven (386, 441–3, 501–2, 568) and the World Tree with its roots in heaven (509), with the underworld (600), with flowering trees (45–48), and with a number of the specific flowers praised throughout the book: tansy (13–16), nasturtium (40–1, 86–90, 634), lotus (181, 441–3), and rose (478–81, 565). Olson evidently repeated his talismanic instruction to himself over and over again, like a mantra or rosary, in order, as Needleman suggests, to study himself, to free himself from concepts, and to transform his life. Through the projectivist community, Olson sought to transmit this idea to other people, with its ethical, epistemological, artistic, and political implications. And he agreed with Needleman's conclusion that, as the poet hints above by alluding to his disclosure of the principle as an act of love, "Incarnated in a great teacher, great ideas become pure energy and love – the teacher acts and lives the ideas; they are his being. The teacher is his knowledge" (Needleman, 42).[11]

By the end of Olson's life, the Black Chrysanthemum came to be the central idea in which he felt himself fully contained. A trio of short poems from the third volume of *The Maximus Poems* will illustrate the point:

> Imbued
> with the light
>
> the flower
> grows down

the air
of heaven
(*Max*, 368)

flower of the underworld

to build out of sound the walls of the city
                                        & display
in one flower   the underworld   so that,

by such means   the unique
            stand forth   clear itself
shall be made known   (*Max*, 600)

        the left hand is the calyx of the Flower
can cup all things within itself, nothing else
there, itself, alone limb of being, acting
in the beneficent air, holding all tenderness
as though it were the soul itself, the Soul's
limb

Sun April 20th 'LXIX (*Max*, 606)

In these three poems we have the Black Chrysanthemum associated with the full range of the spheres of being: heaven, the underworld, and the embodied soul.

In the hospital, as he was dying, Olson took one more opportunity to sum up his doctrine in his last piece of writing, "The Secret of the Black Chrysanthemum." Charles Boer recounts the circumstances of the essay:

> At one point you said to me, "Well, Cholly my boy, it looks like it's over, doesn't it?"
>
> I told you that you couldn't die yet – that there were still a lot of secrets that everyone would like to know.
>
> "There are?" you asked. "What?" . . .
>
> Nor did I know then that, in telling you there were "secrets" we still wanted to know, you would take it as seriously as you did. You started writing a long and final essay, called "The Secret of the

Black Chrysanthemum." It is a remarkable summary of the experience of your life. You placed the manuscript in a sealed envelope,
on the cover of which you wrote, "The 'Secret' notes written this
day December 16th and to be only opened & by Chas. Boer if &
when otherwise still to be retained as mine." (Boer, 149–50)

In this essay-diagram-poem, written on six sheets of paper towel, Olson
sought to work an ultimate alchemy, in which the major ideas, images,
and myths of his life's work were drawn together and transmuted by "the
Golden Pill" of the Black Chrysanthemum.[12] This final synthesis represents Olson's last attempt to contain his knowledge, so that it can be, to
his own work and to that of others, endlessly applicable.

SELF-EXILE AND THE COMMUNITY

Having explored briefly how a secret worked in Olson's life and writing,
we can return again to the social issues. The possession of a secret by an
individual does not spontaneously produce a community; a community
is a social entity, driven by necessities that include but go beyond the
individual. Commenting on the motivations for forming such a community, the sociologist Peter Berger wrote:

> If one cannot transform or sabotage society, one can withdraw
> from it inwardly. Detachment has been a method of resistance to
> social controls at least since Lao-tzu and was made into a theory of
> resistance by the Stoics. The person who retires from the social
> stage into religious, intellectual or artistic domains of his own mak-
> ing still, of course, carries into the self-imposed exile the language,
> identity and store of knowledge that he initially achieved at the
> hands of society. Nevertheless, it is possible, though frequently at
> considerable psychological cost, to build for oneself a castle of the
> mind in which the day-to-day expectations of society can be almost
> completely ignored. And as one does this, the intellectual character
> of this castle is more and more shaped by oneself rather than by the
> ideologies of the surrounding social system. If one finds others to
> join one in such an enterprise, one can in a very real sense create a
> counter-society whose relations with the other, the "legitimate"
> society, can be reduced to a diplomatic minimum. Incidentally, in
> that case the psychological burden of such detachment can be great-
> ly minimized.
>
> Such counter-societies, constructed on the basis of deviant and
> detached definitions, exist in the form of sects, cults, "inner cir-
> cles," or other groups that sociologists call subcultures.[13]

Writing in the early sixties, Berger shared with Olson the hope that new subcultures, formed through resistance and self-constructed ideals, could provide aid and comfort to "religious, intellectual or artistic" exiles from the conformist society of postwar America.

The historical factors that contributed to the existence of the Black Mountain subculture in the fifties and sixties, while real and determinative in themselves, are indicative of broad social, cultural, and artistic issues that have predisposed American poets throughout our history toward the formation of sympathetic communities. When Berger refers to "self-imposed exile" as a social stance, he touches upon a broader concern than the formation of a particular subculture; one could denominate self-imposed exile as a constitutive quality of the American character itself. Although there is no winning an argument about whether Americans are more alienated than anyone else, one can state with conviction that people have come to America, for the most part, by consciously exiling themselves from a native land. A country formed through self-imposed exile bears the marks of this formation in many spheres. As Berger mentions, although one carries into exile "the language, identity and store of knowledge that he initially achieved" elsewhere, one must pay a "considerable psychological cost" for building a new "castle of the mind." Albeit the most effective way for reducing this "psychological burden" is to "find others to join one in such an enterprise," the formation of a subculture – which in the case of America itself has become a dominant society – does not remove the burden altogether. We still retain a myth of exile at the core of the American character: We believe that while other people are at home – supported by social, political, and cultural traditions and grounded in metaphysical certainties – *we* are in exile.[14] As a result of this myth, we feel there is "something missing" in America, something lost, something central to human culture that we have gone without. Looking at the rest of the world, we imagine that, for all our "limitless" freedom and opportunity, other people have found life easier because its meaning has been authorized by an embracing tradition, while we have been left out in the cold.

Within a society that was formed initially as a subculture through self-exile, this gesture of self-exile reoccurs over and over again. In the case of poetry, for instance, self-exile is one of the standard postures assumed by our poets. Moreover, as Berger suggests, the self-exile of a poet is much easier to bear if one can gather a group of like-minded others into a community. The more "innovative," "experimental," or "radical" the poetry, the more likely its practitioners are to form themselves into a network for mutual support. Notable examples of American poetic communities are the transcendentalists, the modernists, the objectivists, the projectivists, the Beats, the San Francisco Renaissance, the New York School, the various ethnic and feminist poetic communities of the last thirty years, and the Language poets.[15] Every one of these groups was created by individuals in self-exile, who banded together around a few rough-and-ready ideas, hoping thereby to overcome some of the isolation, anxiety, and uncertainty about whether it was even possible to *begin* to write poetry in the land of "something missing."

On a further sociological note, it appears that the subcultures with the most power of social bonding are those with the clearest sense of a strong leader, of one individual who articulates the basic articles of belief for the group as a whole. I am not claiming that better poetry is written in a social situation dominated by a leader but merely noting that the doctrinal support offered by the community is more decisive and embracing in certain circumstances. Of the communities mentioned above, those with an acknowledged leader were the transcendentalists (Emerson), the objectivists (Zukofsky), and the projectivists (Olson). In the case of the projectivists, Robert Duncan testifies that, "For all of the poets who matter to me in my generation Charles Olson has been a Big Fire Source" (*Muth* I, 63). Although other poetic communities have been organized less dramatically around a single leader, they can still be seen to manifest a wide variety of forms of social support: such as friendship; the publishing, reviewing, and teaching of one another's work; contributing to each other's economic benefit; and actively engaging in doctrinal discussion. In the case of the communities with strong leaders, the members most often define themselves and their writing against the example of the leader, while in those less dominated by a leader the members define their identities through a wider range of oppositions and examples. The one borderline community in this scheme would be the modernists, most prominent among whom were Ezra Pound, William Carlos Williams, H.D., T. S. Eliot, Marianne Moore, Hart Crane, Wallace Stevens, and Gertrude Stein. Although it may seem too heterogeneous to be so designated, this community's identity could be clarified by dividing it into two parts: a subcult, in which Pound most often took the role of leader, and the several individuals for whom Pound was not a decisive figure – Moore, Crane, Stevens, and Stein. Groups that gravitate around a leader more often possess a secret and also recognize the function of initiation in extending the subcultural circle.

Whether led by a strong figure or not, these American poetic communities succeed, on the whole, in avoiding the sectarianism Olson shuns in "Against Wisdom as Such." The individual poet must, Olson counsels, be "fierce" in insisting "that there are no symbols to him, there are only his own composed forms, and each one solely the issue of the time of the moment of its creation, not any ultimate except what he in his heat and that instant in its solidity yield" (*HU,* 69). This echoes the statement by Emerson in his inaugural essay for American poetry, "The Poet": "But the quality of the imagination is to flow, and not to freeze. . . . Here is the difference betwixt the poet and the mystic, that the last nails a symbol to one sense, which was a true sense for a moment, but soon becomes old and false. For all symbols are fluxional; all language is vehicular and transitive, and is good, as ferries and horses are, for conveyance, not as farms and houses are, for homestead" (*RWE,* 322).

Not only do these poets argue for a temporal rather than an eternal formulation of the group secret, they also demand an individual rather than a universal embodiment of it. Although the secret is a communal possession, it always appears in American poetic communities as a version of the idea of organic form, which by its nature stresses the work of the individual poet in a particular moment. Along this line, the poetic community also functions like a team, in which it is essential for each member to play a different though complementary role. One might well say that the healthier the community, the more diverse and unique the styles and subjects of its members. Because of this, critics can become confused by looking in the wrong direction for family resemblances among members. The strongest use of a community by a poet is not for the definition of a style or a subject but as a mobile, continually renegotiated ground that authorizes self-definition, often through internal differentiation among the members of the group and through external exclusion.

In the case of the Black Mountaineers – Olson, Creeley, and Duncan – the latter two acknowledge deriving a large measure of the authority for their poetry from Olson's "Projective Verse," and yet the poetry written by each of the three poets during their close, twenty-year association differs stylistically, temperamentally, and intellectually from the others as radically as one could possibly imagine. The group maintains cohesion through both external and internal relations: externally, the projectivists defined themselves in opposition to the "academic" poetry represented most conveniently in the Hall, Pack, and Simpson anthology, *New Poets of England and America* (1957);[16] internally, they maintained cohesion through the intensity of their interactions, which formed a complex dynamic of mutual support, criticism, rivalry, and self-assertion. In the course of their voluminous letters to each other, of their infrequent periods of direct association (at Black Mountain College, in San Francisco, at the Vancouver and Berkeley Poetry Festivals [1963, 1965], and at SUNY Buffalo), and of their reviews of each other's work, these poets came for a time to be each other's closest, most devoted, and most influential readers.[17] One could trace in great detail, for example, such productive interactions as the following: the joint creation of an esthetic through letters by Olson and Creeley in the early fifties, for which Olson was so grateful that he dedicated the first volume of *The Maximus Poems* to Creeley as "The Figure of Outward" (*Max, 3*), feeling that he had received "from one man / the world" (*Max, 56*); Duncan's recurring meditations on and responses to "Against Wisdom as Such"; the "permission" Creeley felt he received from Duncan to explore Romanticism and psychology; and the times the poets supported each other against hostile criticism.[18] Robert Duncan once told me that he wrote always with a sense of the other two writing alongside him. This meant, he said, that there were subjects he felt he did not need to cover; but, more importantly, it meant an expectation of his work being read alongside and illuminated by that of the others. Jed Rasula presents a forceful image of the projectivist group as contained within the "field," an image first invoked by Olson in "Projective Verse" and then extended by Duncan in *The Opening of the Field*:

> the notion of composition by field has not, academically speaking, meant what it should. Olson, Creeley, and Duncan did not propose field in the plural (we don't have simple tracts, zoned as Duncan's meadow, Creeley's orchard, Olson's pasture, side by side). *Field* is singular: compositions within the established dynamics of the field are mutual.
>
> No one has yet insisted on a comprehensively intertextual reading of these poets *by field*. Yet the field itself is fully there. The open convolutions of *The Maximus Poems* have Creeley's practice implicit throughout, like cow-parsley in a Massachusetts meadow. There are poems by Creeley one would be delighted to find printed, just so, intercollated in a text of *The Maximus Poems*. They are contributions to a collaborative worksite. These were not poets writing *to* one another (Shelley and Byron did that), but bringing themselves in their practice to an articulate mutual locality.[19]

Although this study does not offer the kind of juxtapositional anthology that Rasula recommends, it does explore their "collaborative worksite" in the hope of revealing more clearly how a poet situates in and is situated by the "field." As we have begun to discover, the field is at one level a nest of particulars in which self-exploration can be conducted, toward the end of regarding one's territory from the vantage point of a witness. On another level, the field is a contained social space, in which the resistant individual enters the resistant community through the agency of an initiatory secret. In the next section I would like to consider what Olson calls "composition by field," in order to see how Olson joins Thoreau in using a poetics of containment.

Chapter 4

THE POETICS OF RECOGNITION

"IF MEN CONSTRUCTED THEIR DWELLINGS WITH THEIR OWN HANDS"

So far, we have looked at containment primarily as an attitude toward one's own life and toward participation in a community. When we move from attitude to action, as Olson consistently urges us to do, then we find that contained action (whether fishing, politics, or art) involves the construction of a container. Just as God, in Thoreau's imagination, walled in Walden Pond for the purpose of containing a portion of heaven on earth ("White Pond and Walden are great crystals in the surface of the earth, Lakes of Light" [*W*, 133]), so we too can build artistic, political, or economic containers for capturing light. For many American poets, including Thoreau and Olson, the form of containment appropriate to writing has come to be called "organic form" – meaning, in general terms, a form created to fit a specific occasion. Starting with Emerson's famous formulation of poetry as "a metre-making argument" ("The Poet," *RWE*, 310), organic form has been construed in America in many ways. Most loosely, it can be taken as the principle of "anything goes," which is an expression of limitlessness similar to the superstitious credulity that accepts as fact Walden's bottomlessness from not having actively sought its bottom. Again, in this issue of form, one must insist upon first reaching the bottom before any right apprehension of freedom and possibility can arise; the twentieth-century poets who employ organic form – from Pound, Williams, and Zukofsky to Olson, Creeley, Levertov, and Duncan – repeatedly speak of it as a matter of accuracy, exactness, unwavering attention, and complex organization.

For Thoreau, form is organic in that it issues from self-containment and then becomes a further container for renewed acts of self-containment. Many of Thoreau's remarks about organic form can be found in the section of "Economy" in which he describes building his

73

house. In the first place, the organically formed house grows from the inside out. But isn't this just a sanction for every variety of self-expression? Not for Thoreau. He makes it clear that the well-formed house arises only from the self-contained individual and becomes, in its turn, the site of self-contained living:

> What of architectural beauty I now see, I know has gradually grown from within outward, out of the necessities and character of the indweller, who is the only builder, – out of some unconscious truthfulness, and nobleness, without ever a thought for the appearance. . . . The most interesting dwellings in this country, as the painter knows, are the most unpretending, humble log huts and cottages of the poor commonly; it is the life of the inhabitants whose shells they are, and not any peculiarity in their surfaces merely, which makes them *picturesque;* and equally interesting will be the citizen's suburban box, when his life shall be as simple and as agreeable to the imagination, and there is as little straining after effect in the style of his dwelling. (*W,* 31–2)

Thoreau disapproves of "the citizen's suburban box" because it is built for show, in order to impress his neighbors. When, through poverty or philosophy (which Thoreau calls "voluntary poverty"), the builder is unconcerned with pretense or show, then the dwelling automatically acquires character – the character, that is, of "the indweller." When Thoreau speaks of the indweller, "who is the only builder," he refers, somewhat slyly, to the witness, the one who dwells in the body but remains fully conscious and detached. The "necessities" of the witness are spontaneous and unpremeditated, producing a building in which there is "little straining after effect in the style." Pursuing the discipline of self-containment, a "builder" approaches "simplicity," in which the "indweller" guides all action by recognizing what will suffice in the present moment. Without plan and without ornament, the mysterious witness constructs the form most fitting for whatever necessities reveal themselves. The form fits both the dweller *and* the function:

> There is some of the same fitness in a man's building his own house that there is in a bird's building its own nest. Who knows but if men constructed their dwellings with their own hands, and provided food for themselves and families simply and honestly enough, the poetic faculty would be universally developed, as birds universally sing when they are so engaged? But alas! we do like cowbirds and cuckoos, which lay their eggs in nests which other birds have built, and cheer no traveller with their chattering and unmusical notes. . . . I never in all my walks came across a man engaged in so simple and natural an occupation as building his house. (*W,* 30–1)

Like Olson in "I, Maximus of Gloucester, to You," Thoreau uses the image of a bird's nest to represent the nurturing qualities of self-containment. Further, he distinguishes two kinds of nest-dwellers with their two kinds of songs. The builder of an organic form gains the right, by dwelling in that form, to sing the song of unself-conscious self-sufficiency. The nest-robber, who inhabits a form that was built for necessities other than its own, must "chatter" endlessly to compensate for its lack of "fitness" in its nest. Finally, it is important to remember the worldly quality of self-contained building: when discussing the form of a nest, a house, a poem, or clothing (*W,* 14–18), Thoreau speaks not of invention from "whole cloth" but rather of assembling materials from many locations in order to construct a container appropriate to a particular place and time. In his disdain for the cuckoos who "lay their eggs in other nests," he expresses his aversion to tradition as the given; on the other hand, he recognizes the difficulty of building without such a tradition when he testifies that "I never in all my walks came across a man engaged in so simple and natural an occupation as building his house."

In his fable of the artist of Kouroo (*W,* 216–17), Thoreau offers a parable of the kind of attention necessary to achieve the simplicity capable of producing a truly sufficient form. The artist sets out to carve a staff with such "singleness of purpose and resolution" that he steps outside of time and produces a creation commensurate with the Creation itself: "He had made a new system in making a staff, a world with full and fair proportions" (*W,* 216). He had, in Olson's terms, created an object that "exists through itself," producing its own self-measure. Thoreau's comment upon this fable of grounding is that "No face which we can give to a matter will stead us so well at last as the truth. This alone wears well" (*W,* 217). But what sort of truth gives us good wear in the form of a work of writing? For both Thoreau and Olson, it must be the recognition of a fact, arising from a "singleness of purpose and resolution," and expressed in an organic form. When Olson, for instance, offered critical judgments of the work of other poets, he seldom awarded them the durable appellation of "true." Charles Boer observed Olson expressing his partial approval in phrases like,

> "A handsome piece of work." "Handsomely done." "A very handsome job." This word described what you thought most other people worked at their art for – a kind of cleverness, subtlety, or well-wrought craft. For others, poetry was the art of expressing oneself "handsomely." Your own work was of another order altogether. The proper response to it was some expression of surprise or disbelief or astonishment at the discovery of some "fact." "Beautiful" was never the right adjective for someone to use as a description of your work. (Boer, 64)

Surprise, disbelief, and astonishment accompany the experience of "recognition" – of rightness or fitness, of seeing anew what one already "knows" – which feels like "truth." In the late lecture, "Poetry and Truth" (1968), Olson revealed that he had always wanted to match Goethe's *Dichtung und Warheit* with a disquisition of his own upon the necessary interdependence of these two terms. And in the 1959 "Letter to Elaine Feinstein," Olson makes clear his own vision of the relationship of beauty to truth; he does not dismiss beauty but sees it as a property of the fact, subordinate to truth: "I believe in Truth! (Warheit) My sense is that beauty (Schönheit) better stay in the thingitself" (*SW*, 27).

"A WHOLE SERIES OF NEW RECOGNITIONS"

In his first platform essay, "Projective Verse" (1950), Olson refers to facts as "objects" and proposes a version of objectivism that he calls "objectism." We have considered earlier how the contained individual must regard him- or herself as an object among other objects, in order to escape "the mud and slush of opinion, and prejudice, and tradition, and delusion, and appearance" (*W*, 66). As Olson puts it, "Objectism is the getting rid of the lyrical interference of the individual as ego, of the 'subject' and his soul, that peculiar presumption by which western man has interposed himself between what he is as a creature of nature (with certain instructions to carry out) and those other creations of nature which we may, with no derogation, call objects" (*SW*, 24). Objectism also extends into poetics: the facts that appear in a poem must be regarded as objects in the same way as objects in the world or persons must be; in the poem, though, as opposed to the world, the poet is responsible for creating the entire context in which the objects exist and interact (which responsibility Olson calls "composition by field" [*SW*, 16]):

> The objects which occur at every given moment of composition (of recognition, we can call it) are, can be, must be treated exactly as they do occur therein and not by any ideas or preconceptions from outside the poem, must be handled as a series of objects in field in such a way that a series of tensions (which they also are) are made to *hold,* and to hold exactly inside the content and context of the poem which has forced itself, through the poet and them, into being. (*SW*, 20)

The facts of the poem are objects that occur through a process of "recognition," which, as Olson suggests, is the proper name for the sort of composition he wishes to define. The process of recognition not only identifies objects but also acknowledges their relations to one another, creating a field of maximum interplay. The tension between the objects of the poem is not an isometric one that immobilizes the objects (to make an analogy to a once popular form of static exercise in which muscles are directly opposed to one another in order to create tension), but instead it is generated through an interplay that respects the self-contained, re- sistant quality of each object: "each of these elements of a poem can be allowed to have the play of their separate energies and can be allowed, once the poem is well composed, to keep, as those other objects do, their proper confusions" (*SW*, 21).

The process of recognition is the central quality of projectivist poetics. When he announces this process in a crucial formulation, however, Olson causes unnecessary confusion by calling it "perception" instead of "rec- ognition." After a short preamble, he begins "Projective Verse" by offer- ing the three "simplicities" of projective verse: the "kinetics," the "prin- ciple," and the "process" (*SW*, 16–17). These three "simplicities" are not easily separable one from another because they all involve the same poetic stance: whether he states emphatically that "FORM IS NEVER MORE THAN AN EXTENSION OF CONTENT" (the principle) or whether he considers the poem as the middle term of an energy transfer from poet to reader (the kinetics) or as a record of instantaneous perceptions (the process), the central fact remains that the species of organic form that Olson calls projective verse "involves a whole series of new recognitions" (*SW*, 16). The process of recognition makes possible both the form of the poem and its impact upon the reader.

Olson is so intent upon emphasizing the matter of speed when he defines the "process" with Edward Dahlberg's dictum, "ONE PERCEPTION MUST IMMEDIATELY AND DIRECTLY LEAD TO A FURTHER PERCEPTION" (*SW*, 17), that he allows Dahlberg's term "perception" to stand for his own more characteristic term "recognition." Projective verse, as practiced by Olson, Creeley, Duncan, Levertov, Dorn, or any of the other poets who have entered the Black Mountain poetic community, has never consisted primarily in recording a fast train of perceptions. Dahlberg's dictum might conceivably lead to a verbal sketchbook of momentary flashes or to the concatenated imagery of automatic writing, as practiced by the surrealists. But projective verse bears little resemblance to a wholly per- ceptual poetry or to a poetry of the unconscious; the process it actually exhibits is that of "a whole series of new recognitions," drawn from the widest possible spectrum of perceptions, emotions, dreams, intellectual constructs, texts, and so on. Olson seems to invoke Dahlberg's formula- tion because it, like Creeley's "form is never more than an extension of content," has the ring of a scientific law and because it emphasizes the need for close attention to the moment rather than for generalized reflec- tion:

It means exactly what it says, is a matter of, at *all* points (even, I should say, of our management of daily reality as of the daily work) get on with it, keep moving, keep in, speed, the nerves, their speed, the perceptions, theirs, the acts, the split second acts, the whole business, keep it moving as fast as you can, citizen. And if you also set up as a poet, USE USE USE the process at all points, in any given poem always, always one perception must must must MOVE, IN-STANTER, ON ANOTHER! (*SW,* 17)

As he chronicles the components that enter into this swift process of recognition, "perception" becomes, instead of the master term, one term among others, like "nerves" and "acts." Eschewing the support of tradi-tional forms, the projective poet will create an organic form through the zigzag process of recognition alone: "From the moment he ventures into FIELD COMPOSITION – puts himself in the open – he can go by no track other than the one the poem under hand declares, for itself. Thus he has to behave, and be, instant by instant, aware of some several forces just now beginning to be examined" (*SW,* 16). The poet must remain on the threshold, ready to move in whatever direction the next recognition leads; in the successful use of this process, one recognition opens onto the next, creating an ever-widening field of bottomless facts.

To see why recognition is a more appropriate term for this poetic process than perception, we can consider a treatment of recognition by the hermeneutic philosopher Hans-Georg Gadamer in his *Truth and Method* (1960). In trying to uncover an ontological explanation for art, he seeks a clue in the nature of play. Building upon insights about play in Johan Huizinga's *Homo Ludens* (1944), Gadamer speaks of a "transforma-tion into structure" that occurs in play, which renders play as, in Olson's terms, "that which exists through itself," its own measure. Gadamer contends that play is a transformation into structure because in it both the player and the world lose their conceptual identities: the identity of the player lapses when everyone's primary concern becomes finding out "what is supposed to be represented, what is 'meant' "; the world disap-pears because the structure of play becomes the structure of reality:

Transformation into structure is not simply transposition into an-other world. Certainly the play takes place in another, closed world. But inasmuch as it is a structure, it is, so to speak, its own measure and measures itself by nothing outside it. Thus the action of a drama – in this respect it still entirely resembles the religious act – exists as something that rests absolutely within itself. It no longer permits of any comparison with reality as the secret measure of all verisimilitude. (*T&M,* 112)

This discussion of Gadamer's bears a remarkable resemblance to Olson's working out of his visionary secret, "Everything issues from the

Black Chrysanthemum, and nothing is anything but itself measured so."
Play as a concept provides for Gadamer a key to the way in which art
issues from itself and becomes its own self-contained measure. Parallel-
ing Olson's line of thought, Gadamer claims that because art as play is a
fully embodied structure, raised above comparison with any external
reality, "a superior truth speaks from it." Subsequently, echoing for us a
point that Thoreau made in speaking of the "spectator," for whom life
may appear as a mere drama or a drama may appear as the truth,
Gadamer argues that,

> Even Plato, the most radical critic of the high estimation of art in
> the history of philosophy, speaks of the comedy and tragedy of life
> on the one hand and of the stage on the other, without differentiat-
> ing between them. For this difference is superseded if one knows
> how to see the meaning of the play that unfolds before one. The
> pleasure of drama is the same in both cases: it is the joy of knowl-
> edge. . . . In being presented in play, what is emerges. It produces
> and brings to light what otherwise is constantly hidden and with-
> drawn. Someone who can perceive the comedy and tragedy of life
> can resist the temptation to think in terms of purposes, which
> conceals the game that is played with us. (*T&M*, 112)

Through the activity of play, poetry enters into the withholding of tradition, producing and bringing "to light what otherwise is constantly hidden and withdrawn." Moreover, the detachment achieved by considering
life a game not only graces one with "the joy of knowledge" but it also
protects one from the "designs" of others, fostering the political virtues
to which Olson accords the highest priority, such as alertness and resistance. The alertness and resistance of children to the designs of adults
may be a result of their faith in the primacy of play: "Children," says
Thoreau, "who play life, discern its true law and relations more clearly
than men, who fail to live it worthily, but who think that they are wiser
by experience, that is, by failure" (*W*, 65).

Having established the self-contained nature of play, Gadamer then
proceeds to show how this nature makes recognition possible. Recognition he relates to representation, to mimesis. The problem with the
classical theory of art, says Gadamer, is that we think of representation as
an imitation of something "out there" instead of as a production of what
one knows. By placing the discussion of representation in the context of a
consideration of play, Gadamer can show that imitation itself is a presentation of knowledge rather than a poor replication of an external world:

> But the concept of imitation can be used to describe the play of art
> only if one keeps in mind the cognitive import in imitation. The

thing presented is there. . . . That is the situation basic to imitation. When a person imitates something, he allows what he knows to exist and to exist in the way that he knows it. A child begins to play by imitation, affirming what he knows and affirming his own being in the process. Also, when children enjoy dressing up, as Aristotle remarks, they are not trying to hide themselves, pretending to be something else in order to be discovered and recognized behind it; but, on the contrary, they intend a representation of such a kind that only what is represented exists. The child wants at any cost to avoid being discovered behind his disguise. He intends that what he represents should exist, and if something is to be guessed, then this is it. We are supposed to recognize what it "is." (*T&M,* 113)

The point of recognition in art, as Gadamer shows by discussing children's disguises, is not to recognize something "real" standing behind the art (the child becomes absolutely indignant when unmasked: this is not "hide-and-seek"), but rather to recognize "what it 'is' " that the art represents. In making this distinction, Gadamer wishes to distinguish art from artifice, and thus from the worship of a form separable from its content: "One does not admire the skill with which something is done, as in the case of a highwire artist. This has only secondary interest. . . . Rather, what we experience in a work of art and what invites our attention is how true it is – i.e., to what extent one knows and recognizes something and oneself" (*T&M,* 114).

Art is true to the extent that it provokes recognition, which is always, as both Gadamer and Olson insist, recognition of something that is and of oneself. Representation is a play of containment, in which recognitions of the world and of oneself occur simultaneously. In recognition we can, as Thoreau says, "be beside ourselves in a sane sense" (*W,* 90). Our ecstasy comes from the fact that recognition is always a gain, an enhancement, a superabundance; it is never merely a restoration of the way things were. Gadamer is careful to make this final distinction:

> But we do not understand what recognition is in its profoundest nature if we only regard it as knowing something again that we know already – i.e., what is familiar is recognized again. The joy of recognition is rather the joy of knowing *more* than is already familiar. In recognition what we know emerges, as if illuminated, from all the contingent and variable circumstances that condition it; it is grasped in its essence. It is known as something. (*T&M,* 114)

This joy accounts for the primary pleasure of art, available to both the artist and the audience. In "A Sense of Measure," Robert Creeley expresses forcefully the central role played by the joy of recognition in his writing: "I am more interested, at present, in what is *given* me to write apart from what I might intend. I have never explicitly known – before writing – what it was that I would say. For myself, articulation is the intelligent ability to recognize the experience of what is so given, in words."[1] For the writer, the epistemological bliss of finding out what one knows through the act of writing is incomparable; the reader, of course, has been proffered the same bliss, although few of us realize that the writer's joy of recognition infuses the text and waits for us to recognize it. As Thoreau reminds us, "The works of the great poets have never yet been read by mankind, for only great poets can read them" (*W,* 70). When we isolate matters of form or taste in our appreciation of a poem, we run the risk of ignoring the poet's truth of recognition. For the poet, the poem is first an act of recognition, a fully embodied game that asks us to recognize what is being represented; the "esthetic" questions that we cultivate in ourselves as "connoisseurs" of poetry have only an incidental, secondary relationship to the truth disclosed in the poem. By focusing too insistently upon what Gadamer calls "aesthetic differentiation," we miss seeing that, in a poem, "that which exists through itself is what is called meaning." Gadamer argues that the correct attitude toward a work of art is "aesthetic non-differentiation":

> It has become clear that what is imitated in imitation, what is formed by the poet, represented by the actor, and recognized by the spectator is to such an extent what is meant – that in which the significance of the representation lies – that the poet's creativity or the actor's prowess as such is not foregrounded from it. When a distinction is made, it is between the material and what the poet makes of it, between the poem and the "conception." But these distinctions are of a secondary nature. What the actor plays and the spectator recognizes are the forms and the action itself, as they are formed by the poet. (*T&M,* 117)

"MAXIMUS TO GLOUCESTER, LETTER 15"

For Gadamer, art is the truth of life because art recognizes what is at play in life. To become a witness, "both in and out of the game" (*LG,* 32), is to recognize one's life as art. Olson agrees with Gadamer that art, as the truth of life, gives one an opportunity to participate directly in recognizing life's meaning: "There is only one thing you can do about kinetic, re-enact it. Which is why the man said, he who possesses rhythm possesses the universe. And why art is the only twin life has – its only valid metaphysic. Art does not seek to describe but to enact" (*SW,* 61). In Gadamer's terms, what art "enacts" is a representation – which can be a representation of anything that is. With its heightened awareness of the process of recognition, projective verse can be seen as a representation of recognition, seeking to provoke the recognition of recognition. This particular representational goal of projective verse accounts for a central formal characteristic found in its various practitioners: a certain kind of disjunctiveness.

There are many kinds of disjunctiveness in modern poetry. Marjorie Perloff has spent a number of years chronicling various sorts in *The Poetics of Indeterminacy* (1981), *The Dance of the Intellect* (1985), and *The Futurist Moment* (1986). A short list of kinds of disjunctiveness and their exemplary practitioners might include: Rimbaud's indeterminate *Illuminations,* calligrams (Apollinaire), cubist poetry (Stein), collage poetry (*The Waste Land*), futurist poetry (Khlebnikov), dada poetry (Tzara), surrealist poetry (Breton), chance poetry (John Cage), Zen poetry (Gary Snyder), and the rhetorical disjunctiveness of John Ashbery. Projectivist poetry is disjunctive in a different way from any of those listed above: it most often records the leaps of recognition from one "fact" to the next. The projective poet moves at the speed of perception, containing the energy of the poem by representing the process of recognition. Reflecting upon the difficulty of containing "at all points energy at least the equivalent of the energy which propelled him in the first place," Olson comments:

> This is the problem which any poet who departs from closed form is specially confronted by. And it involves a whole series of new recognitions. From the moment he ventures into FIELD COMPOSITION – puts himself in the open – he can go by no other track than the one the poem under hand declares, for itself. Thus he has to behave, and be, instant by instant, aware of some several forces just now beginning to be examined. (*SW,* 16)

A poetry that remains aware of "several forces just now beginning to be examined" will be necessarily disjunctive. Instead of looking for formal parallels or symmetry, the poet seeks to contain the energy at play by insisting that one recognition open directly into the next.

If a projectivist poem works, it does so by a method of expansion that grows wider and wider as the trajectory of recognition moves from fact to fact. A relatively clear-cut example for studying this trajectory can be found in "Maximus, to Gloucester: Letter 15" (*Max,* 71–5).[2] The poem starts with a prose passage in which Olson corrects a story from his boyhood about a sea captain who had brought his ship to dock through a snowstorm on Christmas morning (see *Max,* 11, for mention of the earlier version of the story). This prose passage demonstrates Olson's Herodotean ideal of history, in which the facts are coaxed out from the exaggerations of legend. Olson also cares how history is transmitted, reporting from a footnote in his source a conjectural explanation for the inaccuracy: the story was first told by an eighty-five-year-old man, who was recalling an incident from thirty-five years in the past.

The next section of the poem runs as follows:

He sd, "You go all around the subject." And I sd, "I didn't
know it was a subject." He sd, "You twist" and I sd, "I do." He
said other things. And I didn't say anything.

Nor do I know
that this is a rail
on which all (or any)
will ride (as, by Pullman

    that sense the ads are right abt, that you are
    taken care of, you do
    not sleep, you are
    jolted

    And if you take a compartment,
    the whole damned family . . .

I sd, "Rhapsodia . . .
                (*Max*, 72; Olson's ellipses)

In this section of the poem Olson is reflecting upon the very quality of disjunction we have been discussing. Olson's interlocutor is Paul Blackburn, who not long after became associated with the Black Mountain poets. Pondering Blackburn's words, Olson recognizes how his compositional "speed" differs significantly from the speed of a railway train. Olson's unstylish poetry twists and turns, recording the unpredictable movement of his attention as it seeks out recognitions, while a Pullman car purports to deliver one to an advertised destination smoothly and in style. Contrasting his poetry to one of directness, smoothness, and stylishness, Olson opts instead for the essentially paratactic epic method of "rhapsody," whose etymological sense of "songs stitched together" he plays upon.[3] A "seamless" poetry gives the illusion of perfection through formal means, covering over the process of recognition. Olson's method, on the other hand, calls attention to its acts of recognition, letting the seams show in an effort to represent more fully how recognition works.

The most glaring seam in the poem, thus far, occurs between the opening prose discussion of Captain Bowditch and the passage quoted above. If the first passage is about the importance of getting the facts right, no matter how "prosaic" that may render a story, the second picks up with the recognition that such a method of preferring truth to form is going to upset people and to appear "antipoetic" in an age whose primary esthetics is one of comfort. The first passage records Olson's realization, gained through reading a book, that a central story of his childhood needs revision. The second acknowledges that such revisionary writing will always appear unsettling and difficult. Olson praises difficulty as something not to eliminate but rather to accept – as he had earlier in *The Maximus Poems* celebrated a leaky faucet: "the blessing / that difficulties are once more" (*Max,* 18). In the poem above, he first contrasts this resistant difficulty to a direct delivery by rail – much as Thoreau, who, after a long discussion of the "possible" benefits of the railroad in the "Sounds" chapter of *Walden,* dismisses it by saying that he prefers to conduct his life at cross-purposes to such "improvements": "I cross it like a cart-path in the woods" (*W,* 82). Olson then thinks of riding the railroad as a passenger, comfortably pampered in a Pullman car; this brings to mind the subject of advertising, which becomes a central issue for this poem, as for many of the early Maximus poems.

At this point, though, rather than launch into his tirade against advertising, Olson follows a pun on the title of John Smith's "ADVERTISEMENTS For the unexperienced Planters of *New-England,* or any where. . . ." In Olson's estimation, Smith's "ADVERTISEMENTS" offer the real thing – a true, firsthand view not only of the America of 1630 but also of the difficulties encountered by anyone who sets out to tell the truth rather than, as in our present form of advertising, pander to fantasy. As an act of homage, Olson quotes Smith's epigraphic poem, "The Sea Marke," in its entirety. Based upon bitter economic and political experience, the poem delivers admonitory counsel: "If in or outward you be bound, / do not forget to sound." Although as an adventurer Smith made a fatal mistake in forgetting to "sound" the English powers that were, Olson views him as a "watershed" writer who, because of his exploratory triumphs and their true representation in his writing, became simultaneously the last English writer and the first American writer. Olson calls him "that great successor to William Shakespeare" and treasures him, as does Charles Reznikoff, for his clear-eyed description of the wonders of precolonial America.[4] Olson prizes Smith not only for the accuracy of his descriptions of the North American coast but also for his attempt at economic intervention: Smith wanted economic control of New England, but it was given instead to the Puritans, whom Olson credits with founding an America of capitalist exploitation.

The section of the poem following the quotation of Smith's "Sea Marke" opens with the recognition of Smith's importance. "And for the water-shed, the economics & poetics thereafter?" Olson asks, and then launches into his delayed tirade against advertising and Ezra Pound's complicity in it. Having heard Pound praise advertising as good poetry, Olson connects Pound's fondness for the vernacular, and for Villon's skill at using it in poetry, with the insinuating vernacular of advertising as employed by an ad agency (lampooned as "Barton Barton Barton Barton and Barton"); a department store ("Raymond's, Boston"); and Elbert Hubbard (1856–1915), a visionary crank who wrote an influential article addressed to "you Advertising Hustlers." Whereas Pound found his watershed in a picturesque reconstruction of the Quattrocento ("Brer Fox, / Rapallo / Quattrocento-by-the-Beach, # / 429"), Olson finds his in the inquisitive, matter-of-fact John Smith. Finally, Olson's revisionary recognition links Pound's emphases on the vernacular and on melopoeia to the disastrous ascendency of consumerism in contemporary America:

> (o Statue,
> o Republic, o
> Tell-A-Vision, the best
> is soap. The true troubadours
> are CBS. Melopoeia
>
> > is for Cokes by Cokes out of
> > Pause   (*Max*, 75)

Following these lines, the last short section of the poem seems to continue the tone of heavy sarcasm:

> (o Po-ets, you
> should getta
> job
> (*Max*, 75)

If we read these lines in the same sarcastic tone as those preceding them, then the hyphenation of "po-ets" reiterates the cuteness of melopoeia, which renders poets fit only for work in advertising. However, in the light of Olson's earlier praise of that "working poet" John Smith, we must also acknowledge that he simultaneously delivers these instructions with utter seriousness. The real work of the poet, such as Smith engaged in, involves the recognition of how things actually are – a far cry from pandering to the comfort or consumption of "the public." Like Pound, Olson insists upon a direct relationship between poetry and economics, but whereas Pound wishes to found an economic order that will foster the glories of poetry, Olson wishes the poet to participate in the economics of care and attention that render any form of resistant work praiseworthy.

Reading "Letter 15" according to the projectivist poetics of recognition, we can see the progression an Olson poem often follows – from an initial contemplative stance toward deeper and deeper involvement. "Letter 15" begins with a detached, bemused sifting and pondering of facts about Bowditch's Christmas heroics; the tone becomes a bit more feisty when Olson defends himself against Blackburn's objections to his "twisting" style; irony takes hold as Olson presents Smith's bitter poem "The Sea Marke"; Olson reaches an uncomfortable intensity of sarcasm and mockery in the oedipal contest with Pound that accompanies his tirade against advertising; finally, the burning sarcasm seems to wither and then cool into dogma (generally a positive term for Olson) in the last stanza advising poets to get a job. According to Olson's poetics, the increasing heat and speed of the poem assure that the poet is driving it toward the fullest recognitions he or she is capable of. This rising intensity keeps the poem "at all points, . . . a high energy-construct and, at all points, an energy-discharge" (SW, 16). Rather than a falloff of intensity, the final stanza marks a rhetorical shift that subsumes the climactic force of the previous section and projects it outward toward the reader as a charge to meaningful action (whether or not one is a poet).

"HE GOES TO WAR WITH A PICTURE"

To build a "high energy-construct" like "Letter 15" involves resolute containment, so that the heat will not leak out. Since a poem "is energy transferred from where the poet got it (he will have some several causations), by way of the poem itself to, all the way over to, the reader" (SW, 16), then one must practice containment at every stage, from the reception of energy to its composition and publication. The first stage is crucial because the attitude we have toward the world we perceive determines what we are capable of saying:

> I equally cannot satisfy myself of the gain in thinking that the process by which man transposes phenomena to his use is any more extricable from reception than reception itself is from the world. What happens at the skin is more like than different from what happens within. The process of image . . . cannot be understood by separation from the stuff it works on. Here again, as throughout experience, the law remains, form is not isolated from content. (SW, 61)

Once reception takes place, then what has been received is "worked on" and returned again to the world. This all must happen under the pressure of the maximum containment possible, so that what is received will not be dissipated. Olson insists that, "If man is once more to possess intent in his life, and to take up the responsibility implicit in his life, he has to comprehend his own process as intact, from outside, by way of his skin, in, and by his own powers of conversion, out again" (*SW*, 61).

Only by keeping the process intact do we become able to act in a forceful and appropriate way with regard to the present occasion. In Olson's ethics, the ability to act is crucial, so crucial that poetry receives its sanction ultimately as a form of action. All human action, even the writing of poetry, occurs in a specific context; Olson counsels that for effective action one must seek the grounding that comes from regarding oneself in context:

> man's action . . . is the equal of all intake plus all transposing. It deserves this word, that it is the equal of its cause only when it proceeds unbroken from the threshold of a man through him and back out again, without loss of quality, to the external world from which it came. . . . In other words, the proposition here is that man at his peril breaks the full circuit of object, image, action at any point. (*SW*, 62)

Olson's claim for the unbreakable integrity of the "full circuit of object, image, action" repeats in more explicit fashion the hermeneutic circle that Gadamer invokes with regard to representation. Both men are arguing that in any act of representation "what is" remains the same, whether we consider it in the world, in the artist, in the work of art, or in the audience.

Olson focuses particularly upon the senses as initiating this process of representation and action:

> The meeting edge of man and the world is also his cutting edge. . . . if he stays fresh at the coming in he will be fresh at his going out. If he does not, all that he does inside his house is stale, more and more stale as he is less and less acute at the door. And his door is where he is responsible to more than himself. . . . If man chooses to treat external reality any differently than as part of his own process, . . . then he will (being such a froward thing, and bound to use his energy will-nilly, nature is so subtle) use it otherwise. He will use it just exactly as he has used it now for too long, for arbitrary and willful purposes which, in their effects, not only change the face of nature but actually arrest and divert her force until man turns it even against herself. . . . (*SW*, 62)

Olson was one of the first writers to make the ecological statement that how we regard and use ourselves reflects directly upon how we regard and use nature. He may be unique in suggesting that the senses on the surface of the body are the focal points of the relationship between human beings and nature. Olson records this fact as a realization he gained from his stay in Mexico, where he found a still existing congruence of attitude between the contemporary Mayans and their ancient glyphs: "I have found . . . that the hieroglyphs of the Maya disclose a placement of themselves toward nature of enormous contradiction to ourselves, and yet I am not aware that any of the possible usages of this difference have been allowed to seep out into present society" (*SW*, 63). Olson saw this relationship not only in the glyphs but also in the actual surface, the flesh, of the contemporary Mayans:

> When I am rocked by the roads against any of them – kids, women, men – their flesh is most gentle, is granted, touch is in no sense anything but the natural law of flesh, there is none of that pull-away which, in the States, causes a man for all the years of his life the deepest sort of questioning of himself to the wild reachings of his own organism. The admission these people give me and one another is direct, and the individual who peers out from that flesh is precisely himself, is a curious wandering animal like me . . . .
> (*SW*, 57)

The "freshness" of the Mayan stance toward reality (by contrast, Olson compares North Americans to "green-picked refrigerator-ripened fruit" [*SW* 58]), which is still apparent in the way they carry themselves, issued formerly in the invention of their glyphs. Following the lead of Fenollosa's *Chinese Written Character as a Medium for Poetry* (edited by Pound), Olson finds the Mayan glyphs to be a picture-writing so vivid that he (like Pound's friend, the artist Gaudier-Brzeska) can recognize with great force the facts that the words represent:[5] "My assumption is, that these contemporary Maya are what they are because once there was a concept at work which kept attention so poised that . . . they invented a system of written record, now called hieroglyphs, which, on its very face, is verse, the signs were so clearly and densely chosen that, cut in stone, they retain the power of the objects of which they are the images" (*SW*, 58).

Olson seeks a poetics that will keep the attention poised to maintain such an intimately responsive relationship toward the world; he wishes his poetry, likewise, to function as a "glyph" capable of enacting this relationship. He is hardly the first American writer to look toward a form of picture-writing as an interface, like the skin, for uniting nature and creative experience. Using terms such as *typology, hieroglyph,* and *ideogram,* writers and critics have demonstrated the importance of picture-writing in virtually every period of American literature.[6] Thoreau's most sustained exercise in finding the truth in nature occurs in a famous visionary passage in "Spring," where he observes the generation of natural, physiological, and linguistic forms in the melting streams of a sandbank. He concludes his discovery of the interlocking patterns in nature, the human body, and language by stating that nature offers us such facts in hieroglyphics: "Thus it seemed that this one hillside illustrated the principle of all the operations of Nature. The Maker of this earth but patented a leaf. What Champollion will decipher this hieroglyphic for us, that we may turn over a new leaf at last?" (*W*, 203). By learning to read the hieroglyphics, we hope to learn the truth about nature and about ourselves. Perhaps Whitman best sums up this American obsession with trying to read nature as though it expressed moral facts in an ever-fluid Scripture: "To me the converging objects of the universe perpetually flow, / All are written to me, and I must get what the writing means" (*LG*, 47). Choosing the external world as their preferred scripture and claiming their poetry as a hieroglyphic translation of that scripture, American writers seek to ground their work not in a traditional Logos but in nature itself. This strong compensatory desire produces a union of the objectivist and the transcendentalist impulses, a characteristic mode of writing that insists upon the realness of objects while also exploiting their endless interpretability as hieroglyphs.

* * * *

Olson makes use of the figure of the glyph in his poetry in a number of ways. At one level, the poems themselves are offered as glyphs, as self-contained signs that represent simultaneously natural and human truth; like the Mayan glyphs, the poems should "retain the power of the objects of which they are the images." On another level, the colophon to the first edition of the first volume of *The Maximus Poems* (New York: Jargon/Corinth, 1960) calls attention to the figure of Maximus as a glyph. Referring to the graphic image on that edition's title page, the editor (Jonathan Williams? Robert Creeley?) says, "A word on the title-page device: this 'glyph' becomes Olson's 'Figure of Outward,' striding forth from the domain of the infinitely small; and, also, a written character for Maximus himself – the Man in the Word. It is (*really*, like they say) the enlargement of a sliver of perforated tin ceiling found on the floor of a bar room in a ghost town in Arizona. Frederick Sommer made the discovery and the photograph." By calling Maximus "the Man in the Word," the editor implies a contrast to Pound's concept of truth as "man standing by his word." Pound, extending Fenollosa's gloss on the Chinese ideogram for "truth," conceives of truth as a matter of "sincerity," of "unwavering" conviction.[7] Olson's notion of truth is participatory and representational rather than a matter of intention and conviction: one becomes true as a distinct image of human possibility; as an image, one both participates in and represents that possibility.

Olson renders this aspect of Maximus most explicit in his use of the figure of Enyalion. In the 1965 lecture "Causal Mythology," Olson presents Enyalion (a corruption, as he says, of "Enyalios," a Mycenean name for Ares) as an *"imago mundi,"* a picture of the world. The *imago mundi* is something like an internal hieroglyph that each individual carries from birth, an innate perceptual ability through which each person constitutes a world: "Now my argument would be, then, that the way that the Earth gets to be achieved is that we are born, ourselves, with a picture of the world. That there is no world except one that we are the picturers of it. And by the world here I don't mean the Earth, I mean the whole of creation" (*Muth* I, 75). Reaching for truth, each individual bodies forth that "picture" against the prevailing winds of conformity. The *imago mundi* constitutes the individual's unique ability for recognition, for finding out what is; the embodiment of this "picture" comprises the individual's contribution to the world. For Olson, the deepest self-revelation would be a full representation of this picture, of this ability for recognition.

Enyalion becomes the figure of Maximus as recognition, of the god who reveals his shining skin, presents himself as a vulnerable, shimmering membrane – a living hieroglyphic – to the world. Against the Olympian gods, who (like Blake's angels) want to restrain this titanic force in Tartarus, Enyalion goes to war, intent upon reinstating the full range of human possibilities in a time of totalitarian repression:

> rages
> strain
> Dog of Tartarus
> Guards of Tartarus
> Finks of the Bosses. War Makers
>
>   not Enyalion. Enyalion
> has lost his Hand, Enyalion
> is beautiful, Enyalion
> has shown himself, the High King
> a War Chief, he has Equites
> to do that
>
>   Enyalion
> is possibility, all men
> are the glories of Hera by possibility, Enyalion
> goes to war differently
> than his equites, different
> than they do, he goes to war with a picture

far far out into Eternity   Enyalion,
the law of possibility, Enyalion

the beautiful one, Enyalion

who takes off his clothes

wherever he is found,

on a hill,

in front of his own troops,

in the face of the men of the other side, at the command

of any woman who goes by,

and sees him there, and sends her maid, to ask,

if he will show himself,

to see for herself

if the beauty, of which he is reported to have,

is true

he goes to war with a picture   (*Max,* 405–6)

From a composite of Greek, Norse, and Irish mythological elements,
Olson has fashioned a figure to represent the dynamic struggle of projective verse. Enyalion as god of war stands in direct opposition to the
Olympian "War Makers" of our era or of any other: his struggle is
creative rather than destructive, a matter of revelation rather than repression, a vulnerable expansion toward possibility rather than a safe contrac-
tion into the power politics of the status quo. Enyalion struggles to pry
open the lid on human possibility, using a "picture" as weapon. The
picture is both the *imago mundi* and the display of his own naked body;
because he is the fully embodied *imago mundi,* however, these two versions of the picture are really the same. He proves his heroism and his
virility by making himself vulnerable, by stripping naked and facing the
present moment with nothing but his own, innate visionary capacity.
Enyalion, the *imago mundi,* represents the naked, heroic power of recognition resident in each individual ("all men / are the glories of Hera [the
etymology of 'Heracles'] by possibility"), a power that projective verse
summons forth.[8]

At an earlier point in *The Maximus Poems,* before he had constructed the figure of Enyalion, Olson had already equated the power of recognition with stripping naked:

> He left him naked,
> the man said, and
> nakedness
> is what one means
>
> that all start up
> to the eye and soul
> as though it had never
> happened before
> (*Max*, 111)

Stripping down is an act of containment, in which "what one means" is revealed as the nakedness of "that which exists through itself." The freshness of projective verse ("as though it had never / happened before"), like that of the Mayan glyph, is insured by its hewing moment by moment to the unfolding of recognition. The etymology of *recognition* speaks of something known again, but in its deepest nature we experience it as something new, as Gadamer points out: "The joy of recognition is rather the joy of knowing *more* than is already familiar" (*T&M*, 114). American culture strips naked by peeling away layers of custom, reaching for a contained grounding in the unforeseen. Within projective verse, Enyalion as the god of containment provides a sense of measure for the unforeseen: "Enyalion / is in the service of the law of the proportions / of his own body" (*Max*, 406). By making his body a glyph, revealing "what is" by stripping naked, Enyalion creates his own context. In Gadamer's terms, he is the god of a "transformation into structure," which brings a work of art into containment so that we may recognize within it the "fact." The fact shimmers like the god's body, revealing, through its self-contained measure, human possibilities for expansion on the grandest scale. In employing the figure of Enyalion, Olson portrays the paradox of containment and expansion in terms that ground human activity in the earth, while simultaneously revealing the endless transformative possibilities arising from the earth. By grounding himself in the near, Olson discovers a tradition of the far:

> the earth
>
> shines
>
> but beyond the earth
>
> far off Stage Fort Park

          far away from the rules of sea-faring   far far from Gloucester

far by the rule of Ousoos   far where you carry

the color, Bulgar

                    far where Enyalion

          quietly re-enters his Chariot   far

    by the rule of its parts by the law of the proportion

                              of its parts

    over the World   over the City   over man
                                        (*Max*, 407)

Chapter 5

CIRCLES AND BOUNDARIES

"THE REAL HAS JUST THESE BOUNDARIES WE ARE WILLING TO IMAGINE"

Having explored, through the examples of Olson and Thoreau, a multiplicity of ways of approaching the issue of groundlessness, I would like to turn to an adjacent pair of poets, Robert Duncan and Ralph Waldo Emerson, for purposes of comparison and contrast. Thoroughly aware of the self-estrangement by which Americans have relinquished the grounding function of tradition, Emerson and Duncan respond to the lack of a ground not through the discipline of containment but through the "permission" (Duncan's term) of wholeness. Where we found in Thoreau and Olson the paradox of containment and expansion expressed in the vertical figure of the bottomless bottom, a similar but horizontal figure can be seen to superintend the works of Emerson and Duncan: the circle. An image of wholeness, the circle differs from containment by stressing permission (etymologically, "to send through") rather than exclusion ("to close out"); this quality of the circle is most apparent at its boundary, which these poets posit as always subject to reinscription.[1] In this sense, the boundary partakes simultaneously of both wholeness and transgression. By their constant attention to the boundary's liminal function of marking a whole while creating an entryway for that which is outside, Duncan and Emerson replicate the fundamental doubleness we have discovered in tradition itself – that it gives over the world for our inhabitation and, simultaneously, disrupts our complacency through confronting us with the wholly strange.

Beneath a poetic epigraph that promises a "new genesis" through the understanding of circles, Emerson opens his essay "Circles" by declaring the primacy of the circle as a natural and a supernatural figure:

The eye is the first circle; the horizon which it forms is the second; and throughout nature this primary figure is repeated without end.

It is the highest emblem in the cipher of the world. St. Augustine described the nature of God as a circle whose centre was everywhere, and its circumference nowhere. We are all our lifetime reading the copious sense of this first of forms. (*RWE*, 296)

When we think visually, we imagine the circle to be the "first of forms" because it comprises the context in which all other forms are found. In Emerson's world, the eye is the first of senses, and its work is not only visual but visionary; when uncorrupted, the eye looks inward as well as outward: "The sun illuminates only the eye of the man, but shines into the eye and the heart of the child. The lover of nature is he whose inward and outward senses are still truly adjusted to each other; who has retained the spirit of infancy even into the era of manhood" (*Nature, RWE*, 188–9).[2] In *Nature*, Emerson claims that the eye is so essential to the apprehension of truth in nature that nature itself cannot repair its loss. Encircled by the benign woods, "I feel that nothing can befall me in life, – no disgrace, no calamity (leaving me my eyes), which nature cannot repair" (*RWE*, 189). Nature can make whole again everything that is natural. It cannot repair the calamity of the loss of sight because vision goes beyond the natural, and thus constitutes a greater circle; for Emerson, nature would be meaningless, a blank book, without the eyes to read it, to decipher its code.

By taking the eye as the "first circle," Emerson characteristically begins self-reflexively, positing primacy in the act of perception rather than in an object perceived. If we think of the eye as an object, it certainly appears circular, but when Emerson calls it "the first circle" he is referring primarily to the spherical field formed by our stereoscopic vision, as he makes clear by pointing next to "the horizon which it forms." He then repeats this movement from the internal point to the external horizon through his allusion to the famous image of God as being centered everywhere but extending out toward a boundless horizon. The other circle depicted in this passage likewise contains a conjunction of inward and outward: Emerson tells us that "throughout nature this primary figure is repeated without end. It is the highest emblem in the cipher of the world." As something more than a physical form – a hieroglyphic figure in "the cipher of the world" – the circle awaits the human attempt to decode or read it.

So, just what "copious sense" does Emerson find in the circle? Is it truly a figure in cipher, whose solution a determinate key will reveal? Well, not exactly. Rather than disclosing a hidden teaching of which it is merely "symbolic," the circle functions as an emblem that teaches us about circles, about circling. The key to the meaning of the circle seems to lie in grammar, in learning to read "circle" as a verb rather than as a noun: Not a sign of fixed enclosure, of permanent containment, Emerson's circle is emblematic of action, of process. When reading under the sign of the circle, we recognize the fluid, successive character of life, learning to relinquish our admiration for fixity, security, and accomplishment and instead resolving to pursue the heady, challenging truth that "every action admits of being outdone. Our life is an apprenticeship to the truth, that around every circle another can be drawn; that there is no end in nature, but every end is a beginning; that there is always another dawn risen on mid-noon, and under every deep a lower deep opens" (*RWE*, 296).

For Emerson the circle describes a whole, a whole that is apprehended as such by a consciousness (whether individual, collective, or divine) but that must be recognized as never more than provisional – for the circle makes a boundary, a boundary that inevitably must be transgressed. "Permanence is a word of degrees. Everything is medial. Moons are no more bounds to spiritual power than bat-balls" (*RWE*, 297). The act of apprehension, of understanding (called by philosophy the "hermeneutic circle") involves circling, but every circle achieved by understanding proves itself merely the boundary for a new understanding to traverse:

> There is no outside, no enclosing wall, no circumference to us. The man finishes his story, – how good! how final! how it puts a new face on all things! He fills the sky. Lo! on the other side rises also a man, and draws a circle around the circle we had just pronounced the outline of the sphere. Then already is our first speaker not man, but only a first speaker. His only redress is forthwith to draw a circle outside of his antagonist. (*RWE*, 297–8)

Acts of understanding and interpretation comprise an agonistic contest – in which we fight with circles – crossing frontiers, transgressing boundaries, struggling to incorporate, to appropriate the other into a circle of our own devising. Circle falls to circle in the Heraclitean strife of conflicting interpretations. In this grammar of circling, even the most authoritative texts, the "Greek letters . . . are already passing under the same sentence," for Greek thought is not immune to the flux but also comes "tumbling into the inevitable pit which the creation of new thought opens for all that is old. The new continents are built out of the ruins of an old planet; the new races fed out of the decomposition of the foregoing. New arts destroy the old" (*RWE*, 296).

For both Emerson and Duncan, circling is an activity at once creative and destructive. Like tradition, circling brings us first into intimate contact with all the "givens" in the world, only to goad us to refuse their givenness by transgressing every boundary and order ever constructed. When a writer undertakes the risky work of circling, he or she invites a visitation from the otherness of tradition – with results that may be more destructive than they are preservative:

> Beware when the great God lets loose a thinker on this planet. Then all things are at risk. It is as when a conflagration has broken out in a great city, and no man knows what is safe, or where it will end. There is not a piece of science, but its flank may be turned to-morrow; there is not any literary reputation, not the so-called eter-nal names of fame, that may not be revised and condemned. The very hopes of man, the thoughts of his heart, the religion of na-tions, the manners and morals of mankind, are all at the mercy of a new generalization. Generalization is always a new influx of the divinity into the mind. Hence the thrill that attends it. (*RWE*, 299–300)

Like Emerson, Robert Duncan finds a divine thrill in this creative de-struction, this Heraclitean conflagration that consumes all forms in order to think them anew. In a primary statement about his poetry, Duncan proclaims, "I make poetry as other men make war or make love or make states or revolutions: to exercise my faculties at large."[3] And in the poem that ends *The Opening of the Field,* "Food for Fire, Food for Thought," Duncan speaks of the ease with which the poet can cast the world and his own self-conception into the fire that consumes boundaries, all for the sake of a revised conception:

> We are close enough to childhood, so easily purged
> of whatever we thought we were to be,
>
> > flamey threads of firstness go out from your touch.
>
> Flickers of unlikely heat
> at the edge of our belief bud forth.   (*OF,* 96)

Circling represents for Duncan and Emerson a flamey grasping of the whole that is at once encompassing and provisional. Both writers evince an instinctive habit of mind that seeks on the one hand to encompass contradictions and oppositions within the bounds of a single whole, while on the other hand keeping alert to the arbitrary nature of bound-aries; both writers assume that every whole, upon declaring itself as such, tacitly surrenders itself to a greater whole. This paradox of a whole that declares bounds while simultaneously authorizing their transgression bears a strong family resemblance to the paradox of containment and expansion in Olson and Thoreau. Once the bond of kinship between these two methods of alternative grounding is acknowledged, however, we must move to differentiate them, for the "thrill" of circling differs substantially from the discipline of containment. Containment requires separation, a resistance that turns inward; only through this self-enclosure does the poet find possibilities of infinite extension back out into the world. In opposition to the "walled-in" quality of containment, a boundary is a threshold meant by its nature to be traversed. The whole does not contain by exclusion; rather, it encompasses by inclusion, defining a provisional field that grants permission for continual revision. What fascinates Duncan and Emerson is the constant play between the bounded and the unbounded, between form and chaos, between law and freedom. "The Law I Love Is Major Mover," says Duncan portentously in the title of a poem, whose first line continues, "from which flow destructions of the Constitution" (*OF,* 10). Instead of ferreting out and promoting "the facts" as a ground for our individual and communal lives, Emerson attempts to unground, to de-precedent himself, for, as he says, "No facts are to me sacred":

> But lest I should mislead any when I have my own head and obey my whims, let me remind the reader that I am only an experimenter. Do not set the least value on what I do, or the least discredit on what I do not do, as if I pretended to settle anything as true or false. I unsettle all things. No facts are to me sacred; none are profane; I simply experiment, an endless seeker, with no Past at my back. ("Circles," *RWE,* 304)

Although Emerson is disingenuous in claiming to be unprecedented, he tacitly confesses, by capitalizing the term "Past," that he regards it as a primary circle. But the explicit point stands: Both Emerson and Duncan have great faith in spontaneous or gratuitous impulse (which Emerson calls "whim"), and they use it subversively to break through arbitrary boundaries. These writers are impatient with the self-imposed limitations accepted by Olson and Thoreau as a necessary part of the discipline of containment. Using the same image for containment that Thoreau studies throughout *Walden* – the pond – Emerson gives it a negative charge: "Men cease to interest us when we find their limitations. The only sin is limitation. As soon as you once come up with a man's limitations, it is all over with him. . . . Infinitely alluring and attractive was he to you yesterday, a great hope, a sea to swim in; now, you have found his shores, found it a pond, and you care not if you never see it again" ("Circles," *RWE,* 299). For Emerson and Duncan, containment cannot provide an adequate alternative grounding method; they consider it a sterile means of restraint rather than a necessary precondition to expansion. No matter how vigorous or muscular Olson and Thoreau appear in their efforts at containment, these writers do exhibit a certain ponderousness, a pedagogical seriousness, an air of authority born of austerity, which Duncan and Emerson counter by a tone of enthusiasm, abandon, or whimsy, with which they are willing to indulge the impulse of the moment – even to an embarrassing extent – in the pursuit of a hitherto inaccessible insight.[4]

Seeming to speak for both Duncan and himself, Emerson proclaims: "The one thing which we seek with insatiable desire is to forget ourselves, to be surprised out of our propriety, to lose our sempiternal memory, and to do something without knowing how or why; in short, to draw a new circle. Nothing great was ever achieved without enthusiasm. The way of life is wonderful; it is by abandonment" ("Circles," *RWE*, 306). Duncan cultivates this attitude of enthusiasm and abandonment with even greater devotion than Emerson, returning again and again in his criticism, for instance, to defend himself and other poets against critics concerned with propriety. Following his Freudian persuasion, Duncan identifies the voice of propriety as issuing from the superego, which attempts to repress childish impulses and to keep the ego aligned with the reality principle. As a direct affront to the superego – wishing, as Emerson says, to retain "the spirit of infancy even into the era of manhood" (*Nature, RWE*, 189) – Duncan declares himself a partisan of the childish:

> It is a characteristic of my feeling and thought that I have consciously proposed that I would keep alive and at work as primaries earliest experiences and structures. I would not reprove the child in me in my also being adolescent, in my also being grown-up. Hence I seek out and fortify even embarrassing sentiments – sentimentalities they can be seen to be by those critics who have put away childish things. (*FC*, 220)

Not only have they upset decorous critics, but the childish qualities of abandon and enthusiasm in Duncan drove Olson to distraction as well. He was particularly worried about enthusiasm, for it made Duncan seem like a sectary; although Olson wished to form a poetic community, he wanted that community made up of resistant individuals: " 'Contained.' I fall back on a difference I am certain the poet at least has to be fierce about: that he is not free to be a part of, or to be any, sect" (*HU*, 68–9). Olson addressed "Against Wisdom as Such" to Duncan, cautioning him that "only sectaries can deal with wisdom as separable" (*HU*, 68), for they are content to take upon themselves the terms of another's discourse. For the poet, on the other hand, "there are no symbols . . . , there are only his own composed forms, and each one solely the issue of the time of the moment of its creation, not any ultimate except what he in his heat and that instant in its solidity yield" (*HU*, 69). But Duncan maintained that to proscribe the use of traditional wisdom, or even of contemporary foolishness, is to draw the circle of poetry too tightly. Duncan was impatient with Olson's drive for containment and acted the playful heretic within the Black Mountain cult. While teaching at Black Mountain College, for instance, Duncan produced "a dramatic farce, *The Origins of Old Sun,* in which 'Old Sun' was portrayed as an oversized, demanding infant in diapers" (Clark, 255). In "From a Notebook," Duncan muses upon his anti–Black Mountain tendencies; announcing the central Romantic strain in his writing, and claiming a host of writers as ancestral figures whom Olson considered anathema, he declares:

> This series of notes serves to explore a style and temperament in which the Romantic spirit is revived. Back it goes to recent readings again of George MacDonald's *Lilith,* to earlier pleasures and thrills in Coleridge and Poe. But thruout I am conscious of the debt to Wallace Stevens – that there is a route back to the Romantic in Stevens. Then, I discovered . . . Charles Henri Ford's "Anthology of Prose Poetry." Mallarmé's "Penultimate" and Poe's "Shadow" are all of the vein along which I am working again. This is of course the radical disagreement that Olson has with me. In a sense he is so keen upon the *virtu* of reality that he rejects my "wisdom" not as it might seem at first glance because "wisdom" is a vice; but because my wisdom is not real wisdom. He suspects, and rightly, that I indulge myself in pretentious fictions. I, however, at this point take enuf delight in the available glamor that I do not stop to trouble the cheapness of such stuff. . . . I like rigor and even clarity as a quality of a work – that is, as I like muddle and floaty vagaries. It is the intensity of the conception that moves me. (*FC,* 65)

Countering the Poundian virility of Olson's "*virtu* of reality," Duncan chooses a promiscuous "intensity of conception," refusing to practice the "chastity" necessary for amassing such *virtu.* Looking at the opposition between the imaginary and the real in Duncan and Olson, Don Byrd characterizes their quarrel as "the fictionalist versus the literalist."[5] As Duncan and Byrd rightly point out, the differences between Olson and Duncan do not reduce to a disagreement about particular kinds of wisdom: Duncan is eager to adopt all of Olson's wisdom, as he does that of countless other figures; these two poets separate along dispositional lines – the fictive versus the literal, the promiscuous versus the chaste. Duncan envisions the containment Olson achieves through facts not as a prescriptive stance toward reality but as a compelling circle, around which he must immediately draw another circle in order to enact the boundary work of wholeness. In the oxymoronic title of his book of essays, *Fictive Certainties,* Duncan makes clear the priority for his work of fiction over fact. By "fiction" he means an imagined whole, with an internal sense of harmony, order, or fitness, whose certainty is intuitive rather than externally verifiable. The discovery of such an organic order (which may well contradict the factual or social orders in which the materials of the poem are usually found) constitutes the poet's imaginative work. Duncan and Emerson share a "Doctrine of Correspondences,"[6] in which there is "manifold meaning, for every sensuous fact" ("The Poet," *RWE*, 307); the meaning differs from that contained in the fact for Olson and Thoreau because, as Duncan insists, meaning becomes apparent only in relation:

> Facts or ideas or images are not true for me until in them I begin to feel the patterning they are true to, the melody they belong to. Once this feeling of a patterning begins, the work comes to one's hand; the form of the whole can be felt emerging in the fittingness of each passage. I am no longer thinking or proposing ideas but working *with* them, seeing with them, as I work. (*FC*, 31)

For Duncan, as for Stevens (who provided Duncan "a route back to the Romantic" but was reviled by Olson), there is a truth in fiction. However, instead of following Stevens into a meditation upon the always unstable relationship of fiction to reality, Duncan investigates what might be called the structure of fiction itself, finding the truth of fiction in a series of figures for circling. Over and over in his poetry and prose, Duncan engages figures such as the Circle Dance, the Field or Meadow, the Grand Collage, the Museum, the Sentence, the War, and the Symphony – figures of created wholeness that include both cooperation and strife, harmony and discord. Like Emerson, in "Circles," Duncan insists that these figures of wholeness exist simultaneously in the world and in the mind and that they comprise a creative/destructive fiction. The "Grand Collage" composed by these figures of circling differs from the modernist collage of Eliot or Pound because it keeps the frame fluid, open to the constant revision of boundary work. Both Eliot and Pound seek to construct a final collage that will preserve the greatest moments of Western tradition and will create a particular pattern of these moments that authorizes their own poetry; the art of circling in Duncan and Emerson prevents the figures of their Grand Collages from ever achieving a rigid placement, and thus makes more explicit the cooperation between the poet and the past in contextualizing one another. Duncan's most frequently employed figure for the fictive process of circling is "Rime," whose purview he extends beyond the correspondence of sounds to include all sorts of correspondences. In his poem "Merlin" (*RWE*, 461–4), Emerson presents an incipient version of this notion of rhyme, seeing the correspondence inherent in rhyme as the basis of a bilateral symmetry that runs through both nature and human fate. For the last thirty years of his life, Duncan was writing an open-ended series of poems called "The Structure of Rime," in which he investigated how language makes possible these recognitions of correspondence. In the second poem in the sequence, we find a central pronouncement of the law of Rime:

> What of the structure of Rime? I asked.
>
> *An absolute scale of resemblance and disresemblance establishes measures that are music in the actual world.*   (*OF*, 13)

Like Emerson, Duncan works within a Platonic notion of harmony or correspondence, governed by the image of the Music of the Spheres (*"The actual stars moving are music in the real world. This is the meaning of the music of the spheres."* [*OF*, 13]). But like Emerson and in distinction to Plato, Duncan believes that such harmony must be actively discovered by the poet through listening to language, rather than approached through a philosophical discipline of discarding illusions until an immutable truth is reached: "I ask the unyielding Sentence that shows Itself forth in the language as I make it, / Speak! For I name myself your master, who come to serve. / Writing is first a search in obedience" (*OF*, 12). In both Emerson and Duncan there is an Orphic strain wedded to the Platonic, which renders the poet's imagination a participant in the work of creation: from this perspective, Duncan contends that fiction is true (fictive *certainty*) and that the poet's ability to apprehend truth is an artful capacity to keep the story in play, to keep the plot thickening, to read a fictive intent at work in momentary occurrences, and to incorporate as many seemingly contradictory or mutually exclusive elements as possible into an ever-expanding whole. The great power of the fictive imagination, according to Duncan, resides in its bringing into a single story the most heterogeneous aspects of our experience and of the world – not in order to create a final, static synthesis but rather to concatenate the largest series of discrete boundaries:

> My perspective would go throughout time and the present world of man as it extends into an acknowledged nature of our being. In this order I am fascinated by boundaries, by the fact that the real has just these boundaries we are willing to imagine. In my work I do not conceive of image as leading to image, of a stream of consciousness or associations, nor of the development of images, as the primary form, but of the coexistence of many figures: a plurality of boundaries means a multiphasic image of What Is. And to extend that imagination, I study the sciences of Man and His superstitions, I gather in wherever it speaks to me His testimony of experience, searching to have a more and more multitudinous image of what

Man is, and a more and more various resource in His being. (*FC,*
136–7)

The largest whole that Duncan wishes to construct is not a seamless
mesh or an "ideal order" (to use Eliot's notion of tradition) but rather a
multiphasic field, in which innumerable boundaries remain intact while
interrelating. In offering such a whole, with its wildly various "resemblances and disresemblances," Duncan courts a certain bewilderment
in his readers. If one has trouble perceiving the "absolute scale" of the
story as it winds through the incredible "plurality of boundaries" that
makes up Duncan's "multiphasic image," then one risks frustration and
an inability to evaluate the success of this seemingly all-inclusive poetry.
Duncan and Emerson both stretch constantly for the frontiers in a search
for ever-greater wholes, incurring through their inveterate inclusivity
perils that one critic described quite clearly (with reference to Emerson):

> The range of affirmation that can be found in Emerson's work is
> unusually wide. Energies and interests ordinarily opposed are pres-
> ent in an odd though compelling harmony; yet at the same time
> much seems omitted. It is difficult to distinguish, either in principle
> or among particulars, the exciting truth from the trivial illusion, the
> authentic insight from its near self-parody.
>
> And in the midst of one's ambivalence, one's alternations of
> respect and dismissal, trust and boredom . . . Emerson tests his
> critics as few writers do. . . . His serenity, his independence, his
> grace and agility are perpetually escaping the categories of the pro-
> fessionalized intelligence. His wit and conscience threaten the
> cleverness by which the social self conceals its own moral coward-
> ice. Like Lawrence, Emerson has a way of exposing the uncon-
> scious limits and refusals of the very critics who suppose them-
> selves to have identified for correct admiration the essence of his
> achievement.[7]

Although his personal qualities are different from those of Emerson (and
Lawrence) noted above, Duncan's uncanny inclusivity evokes the same, if
not more powerful, reactions: readers vacillate between profound admiration and dismissive incredulity, and yet from either pole there is always
the vaguely uncomfortable sense that, however fully one thinks to have
understood him, Duncan has possibly succeeded in drawing a circle in
which the reader, too, is comprehended.

This sense of comprehensive incomprehension Duncan actively cultivates, both in himself and in his readers, for such trust in a condition of
not-understanding allows one to cross boundaries and to perceive a new
whole.[8] When a poet dwells in boundaries rather than in containment, he

or she practices a readiness, a sense of cooperation with the unforeseen that can be refined to an extremely subtle degree, where unimagined wholes suddenly spring to life from the least likely of boundaries. For Duncan, this dwelling on the boundary is a poetic, epistemological, spiritual, and even political and moral imperative:

> Remembering Schrödinger's sense that the principle of life lies in its evasion of equilibrium, I think too of Goethe's Faust, whose principle lies in his discontent, not only in his search but also in his search beyond whatever answer he can know. Our engagement with knowing, with craft and lore, our demand for truth is not to reach a conclusion but to keep our exposure to what we do not know, to confront our wish and our need beyond habit and capability, beyond what we can take for granted, at the borderline, the light finger-tip or thought-tip where impulse and novelty spring. (FC, 87)

Rather than pursue the security and conviction that arise from a containment within facts known thoroughly, Duncan seeks his ground within a sense of the whole that includes what he does not see or know. Through his trust in the efficacy of fiction, he believes that he can extend his poetry into more and more mysterious regions: "The rimes of this poetry are correspondences, workings of figures and patterns of figures in which we apprehend the whole we do not see" (HD I.3, 67). The understanding that tries to control or manipulate loses, in its very grasping, its hold upon the farthest-flung and most encompassing circles, in which knowledge must include not-understanding: "I am but part of the whole of what I am, and wherever I seek to understand I fail what I know" (FC, 79). As the circling art of wholeness inscribes in poetry what it does not understand, it reaches toward the notion of tradition as "something strange and refractory to interpretation, resistant to the present, uncontainable in the given world in which we find ourselves at home."[9]

"TRANSGRESSING THE REAL"

Circles create boundaries, and boundaries invite traversal. The god of boundaries, Hermes, whose phallic stone herms were worshipped in ancient Greece as boundary markers, holds a special place in Duncan's crowded pantheon of deities and heroes. Hermes is the god of the liminal, of the threshold or margin, who guides the dead to the underworld and bears messages across from region to region among gods and humans. As such he is the hermeneutic god – the translator and interpreter – and also the god of poets, whose lyre he invented. The trickster who breaks the law by stealing Apollo's cattle and then tells charming lies to hide the fact, Hermes likewise is the patron of liars and thieves.[10] In his

Egyptian form of Thoth, he is the god of writing and ancestor to the gnostic Hermes Trismegistus, the bearer of hermetic wisdom. Duncan received his initiation into the worship of Hermes as a child, and in the many allusions to his childhood that appear throughout his prose and poetry, Hermes and hermetic lore are central. Remembering the occult flavor of his childhood, Duncan recalls what he was told of Hermes:

> Hermes, Mercury, was the one with winged helmet and winged sandals I had seen in the bronze figure that stood on the piano at Aunt Fay's. He was the god of the high air, of those helium fields, carrying a rod around which two snakes twisted. This wand or *caduceus* meant, Aunt Fay explained, that he was god of Life, systole and diastole of the heart beat. But the real image of the god was the picture Grandmother showed me in *The Book of the Dead*. Egypt was the hidden meaning of things, not only of Greek things but of Hebrew things. The wand of Hermes was the rod of Moses, and my grandmother studied hieroglyphics as she studied Hebrew letters and searched in dictionaries for the meaning of Greek roots, to come into the primal knowledge of the universe. This god, the Egyptian Thoth, was Truth, the truth of what life is that we know in death. (*HD* I.5, 5)

As a poet, Duncan put to use his childhood hermeneutic training in the puzzling out of occult messages, making it the basis for an intricate, unpredictable art of circling. Charles Olson, however, suspected that a faded, ouija-board spiritualism, nurtured in San Francisco, lay behind Duncan's relentlessly interpretive poetry, and he accused Duncan, in "Against Wisdom as Such," of inhabiting a tawdry world of illusory hidden meanings: Olson complains sarcastically that "San Francisco seems to have become an école des Sages ou Mages as ominous as Ojai, L. A." (*HU,* 68). Duncan defends himself by claiming to be a more devoted follower of Hermes – honoring all of the god's manifestations, through both truth and lies – than were his family in their Hermetic Brotherhood or his friends in their dabbling in magic. In the double nature of Hermes, Duncan finds a key to what he conceives of as the double nature of poetry, its simultaneous wholeness and transgression, "a connexion working in both directions":

> Pound sought coherence in *The Cantos* and comes in Canto 116 to lament *"and I cannot make it cohere."* But the *"*SPLENDOUR, IT ALL COHERES*"* of the poet's Herakles in *The Women of Trachis* is a key or recognition of a double meaning that turns in the lock of the Nessus shirt.
> Hermes, god of poets and thieves, lock-picker then, invented the

bow and the lyre to confound Apollo, god of poetry. "*They do not apprehend how being at variance it agrees with itself,*" Heraklitus observes: "*there is a connexion working in both directions.*" (*BB,* 4)

In a passage from "After Reading *Barely and Widely,*" a poem reflecting upon the verse of Louis Zukofsky, Duncan incorporates Olson's remark about the dangers of San Francisco into a meditation upon the doubled hermetic strain running through his own poetry:

Of such double-dealings I would talk.
Of these are turnd from hostile threads
the round around of a single rope.

Hermes, a cheat and thief, so it is said,
spited out with Aphrodite, shows
the soul through dark ways indeed,

"an école des Sages ou Mages
as ominous as Ojai".
He's the old faker that haunts the page!

not me! that *other* one whose eyes
squint! psychopompos, undertaker,
Thomas the Rimer, Solomon the Wise.

Mercury, the *Liber de arte chymica* says
"is all metals, male and female";
may be within and without the law, day's

child and night's too; may be jew and gentile,
"an hermaphroditic monster even in the marriage of soul and
    body."
The words in the song are *mercurial.*

The poet's art is one of tact and guile, its boundary
limitless only when it's done;
elsewhere seeming almost to flounder

helpless into meaning, by rime
restricted. How are we to follow?
The song circles. . . .   (*OF,* 91)

Under the sway of Hermes, Duncan claims that every truth he finds has a double nature, is both true and false, both real and fictive: "Of these are turnd the hostile threads / the round around of a single rope." (Notice the emphasis on "round," which calls attention to the circling quality of the poetry, referred to again at the end of the quoted passage in "The song circles.") Hermes, himself "a cheat and thief," twines in a hostile manner with Aphrodite, forming an uneasy hermaphrodite, which, though doubled, still guides the soul to the underworld, as Hermes traditionally did (or as did Dante's guide, Vergil, who also "shows / the soul through dark ways indeed" and is likewise both part of and separate from Dante). Picking up on Olson's abhorrence for the esoteric and hermaphroditic scene in San Francisco, Duncan ironically equates it with hell, simultaneously admitting that the double Hermes leads him into this scene but insisting that, by following Hermes, his own poetry becomes imbued with the difficult, double-edged truths of the trickster: "He's the old faker that haunts the page!"[11] Olson fears that Duncan will lose his poetic abilities among the decadent sign-readers of San Francisco, for "the poet cannot afford to traffick in any other 'sign' than his one, his self, the man or woman he is" (*HU,* 69).[12] For Olson, the hieroglyphic impulse in American culture must be contained through exemplary self-inscription, through presenting oneself as a glyph; in San Francisco, he fears, the mode of picture-writing has run riot and thus forfeits its grounding function as an act of containment. In response, Duncan claims that Hermes as "the old faker," who reads "signs" for their esoteric meaning, is "not me! that *other* one whose eyes / squint! psychopompos, undertaker, / Thomas the Rimer, Solomon the Wise."[13] Through his own double vision (which reflects an actual visual impairment: "the double vision / due to maladjustment of the eyes" [*OF,* 45]), Duncan sees that within himself is another (an allusion to Rimbaud's "Je est un autre"), who magically squints at the truth but with whom Duncan does not wholly identify. In admitting his own double, contradictory nature, he refuses to present himself as a fully achieved or exemplary glyph; instead, he insists upon the disruptive, transgressive potential inherent in the wily trickster.

In the next section of the poem, Duncan considers Hermes from an alchemical perspective, in which the god's hermaphroditic nature is not only male and female but "within and without the law." Here Hermes becomes a ripe figure for depicting the ultimate relation of wholeness to transgression in Duncan's boundary art. For instance, in the line, "The words in the song are *mercurial,*" Duncan uses the term "mercurial" in two ways: to portray the operations of his poetry as creating a whole alchemically from disparate materials, and to acknowledge that his poetry constantly changes form through transgressing its own order. But to qualify his poetry as mercurial is not, Duncan argues, to charge it with inconsequence or random mutation. From the boundary god Hermes, the poet learns *how* to traverse boundaries, how to follow the trickster's lead. In this, "The poet's art is one of tact and guile, its boundary / limitless only when it's done;" the poet pays strict attention to where he is being led, finding limitless possibilities, not at the moment of composition, but in the moment of interpretation. The final lines of this passage ("elsewhere seeming almost to flounder / / helpless into meaning, by rime / restricted. How are we to follow?") describe the illusory sense of inadvertence that accompanies the art of wholeness, in which, like a trickster, one inevitably stumbles into meaning and coherence because "the song circles."

* * * *

Inviting the hermaphroditic god of boundaries to oversee his life and work, Duncan upsets not only his fellow projectivist Charles Olson but also strict, single-visioned occultists, such as those who surrounded him in his childhood. For Duncan, poetry itself is a determinative world, in which "an absolute scale of resemblance and disresemblance establishes measures that are music in the actual world" (OF, 13). Turning his back on the truth of facts and also the truth of esoteric wisdom, Duncan seeks to escape into a truth of poetry: "Working in words I am an escapist; as if I could step out of my clothes and move naked as the wind in a world of words. But I want every part of the actual world involved in my escape. I bring the laws that bound me into an aerial structure in which they are unbound as outlines of a prison unfolding" (BB, v). Trying to free himself of the world by transposing its structures into poetry, he runs the risk of hiding from the world. Throughout his life and work, Duncan asserted the primacy of poetry over all other endeavors. One liability he incurred was to be perceived as a "poet's poet." But there are psychological dangers as well in his rendering the world fictitious.

In his teens, Duncan made a radical break from the middle-class, professional world of his parents, choosing to become a poet rather than follow his father in the practice of architecture: "my conversion to Poetry was experienced by myself and by those about me as my being at war with every hope the world before had had of me. Poetry was not in the order of things. One could not earn a living at poetry. Writing poems was not such a bad thing, but to give one's life over to poetry, to become a *poet,* was to evidence a serious social disorder" (FC, 112). By rejecting the conventional world around him, Duncan repeated the ungrounding gesture of American culture and precipitated a kind of lifelong identity crisis analogous to that experienced by American poetry as a whole: "The ideal for my middle-class professional parents was to become someone, to have character and individuality, to be a real person and make a name for oneself. They strove to establish their identity in facts and actual achievements and to keep in its place another world of lower desires and idle fancies" (FC, 112–13).

In response to the disapprobation he received from all sides for seeming to step beyond the social fabric, Duncan asserted the primacy of poetry over all other endeavors and developed a whole series of secondary beliefs that directly countered the values held by his parents' world. Not only did he reject middle-class law and order through pursuing political anarchism and homosexuality, but he even defended himself against the disciplines that directly fed his own work: He took Freud as a major figure in his lifework but steadfastly refused to be analyzed; he drew primary sustenance from religion, spirituality, and occultism but never professed any religion, sect, or rite; he devoted large portions of time to critical writing and teaching, but he attacked vociferously the institutions of education and criticism and maintained a resolute distance from them.[14]

While taking an anarchist stand in relation to all of the institutions valued by his parents – the protestant work ethic, representative government, heterosexuality and the family, psychoanalysis, religion and esotericism, and professional teaching and criticism – Duncan used his poetry and prose almost exclusively to advocate the autonomy of poetry, to urge his readers to view poetry as a law unto itself that subsumes and transvalues all other realms of life. Ironically, then, one of the dangers of Duncan's poetry of inclusion and permission is a unilateral rejection of the values of those around him. His ability to accept and integrate all the parts of himself is truly remarkable – a kind of psychological tour de force that places him in the company of great self-explorers like Montaigne, Rousseau, Wordsworth, Dickinson, Proust, and Freud – but his shunning of the world of convention is also compensatorily extensive and results in a kind of self-enclosure that can at times encourage a bathetic self-indulgence. The third facet of Duncan's character worthy of mention in this portrait of an identity in perpetual crisis is the autodidact, engaged in a vast study and appropriation of Western poetry; of world mythology, mystery religions, and mysticism; of psychology; and of the broad outlines of modern science – all of this forming the material for an idiosyncratic tradition that is broader and more inclusive than that of any other American poet.

Like Emerson and Whitman, Duncan consistently imagines a self that extends beyond individual identity. In a lecture entitled "The Self in Postmodern Poetry," Duncan remembered how in his childhood he realized that self-knowledge "was the one necessary thing and that it was the key to seeking knowledge that lay beyond knowing, the one truly existing beyond one was this 'self'" (*FC*, 223). From Emerson's "Self-Reliance" he quotes a description of the self extending beyond one: "We lie in the lap of immense intelligence, which makes us receivers of its truth and organs of its activity. When we discern justice, when we discern truth, we do nothing of ourselves, but allow a passage of its beams" (*FC*, 227). "Today," Duncan says, "in 1979, reading that essay, I find again how Emersonian my spirit is" (*FC*, 226). Duncan's primary conception of the self – as a site of wholeness with open boundaries rather than as a contained actor – differentiates him markedly from Olson. Self-discovery for Olson is the project of acquiring greater and greater authority and ability for action; self-discovery for Duncan occurs upon a stage on which the most heterogeneous elements are brought into a dramatic enactment. Alongside the dichotomy of the literal and the fictive, we must place that of action and enactment.

Duncan enacts an Emersonian sense of self within his poetry through (as he titles one of his "Passages" poems) "Transgressing the Real." By "transgressing the real" he means turning away from the pressing demands exacted by the real (to which a stable identity can necessarily respond with only partial action) and instead reenacting through poetry the whole scene of conflict that constitutes the real (and, reciprocally, the self). "Transgressing the Real, Passages 27," written during the Vietnam War, pictures the poet as a magician, able to withdraw from the anguished reality of the war into a poem that will, as Allen Ginsberg also hoped to do in "Witchita Vortex Sutra" (1966), magically draw the young men out of combat and into its "celestial cave":

> In the War they made a celestial cave.
> In the War now I make
> a celestial cave,   a tent of the Night
> (the Sun, no longer striking day upon the Earth,
> but light-years away   a diamond spark in the host of stars
> sparkling net   bejewelld wave of dark   over us
> distant coruscations
> "play of light or of intellectual brilliancy"
> in which I pretend   a convocation of powers
> (under the cloak of his poem   *he* retires
> invisible
> so that it seems no man   but a world speaks
> for my thoughts are servants of the stars, and my words
> (all parentheses opening into
> come from a mouth that is the Universe   *la bouche d'ombre*
> (The poet-magician Dr Dee in his black mirror
> calls forth his spirits from their obscurity)
> thru the rays of invisible and visible bodies,
> known and unknown   sources and senders,
> thru fumes, lights, sounds, crystallizations . . .
> For now in my mind all the young men of my time
> have withdrawn allegiance from *this world,* from public things •
> and as their studies in irreality deepen,

industries, businesses, universities, armies
shudder and cease   (*BB*, 120)

The "poet-magician" transgresses the real by opening up a hidden cave within it, where the real is redrawn in miniature as an image of the self. Borrowing from the Orphic cosmogony, Duncan reduces the real to its seed-form, using in *Bending the Bow* a whole family of microcosmic images: the cave (*BB*, 120), the ring (*BB*, 29, 99), the egg (*BB*, 10, 46–7), the moon (*BB*, 17–18), the grail (*BB*, 31–3, 55), and the seed (*BB*, 133). Inside the cave one is protected from outside demands, but on the other hand the forces of the real seem more concentrated and encompassing within its echoing walls. This paradox points out the resemblance of such a poetry to the states of dream or revery, in which we leave the "real" world behind only to confront its forces in a more concentrated form. Borrowing directly the Orphic image of the World-Egg for his "Tribal Memories/Passages 1," Duncan describes the enclosed world as an egg, which is itself "the dream in which all things are living":

I am beside myself with this
          thought of the One in the World-Egg,
    enclosed,   in a shell of murmurings,

                    rimed round
                    sound-chamberd child.
                        (*BB*, 10)

In this passage, the poet leaves the world behind by curling up and turning inward. This gesture constitutes one of the two types of boundary work: the poet can transgress the boundary of a circle by crossing over into a more inclusive whole, showing that which was denied, opposed, repressed, or assumed by the prior circle; or, alternatively, the circle may be dissolved through self-reflexivity, through stepping back as Emerson does from the horizon to the eye that constitutes it. It is this self-reflexive gesture that Duncan makes in "Transgressing the Real," looking inward at the power of sight, as though the eye were to turn back and perceive the skull as a cave. The power gained from such an endeavor is one of self-consciousness, an awareness of one's complete responsibility for everything the eye/I perceives: If the young soldiers could be made to study this "irreality" (as many of them were, through psychedelic drugs), their expanded awareness would, Duncan feels, make it impossible for them to commit the crime of participating in this war.

As a poet, Duncan often transgresses the real by placing himself inside a cave or an egg, like a "rimed round, / sound-chamberd child." In these close quarters, every sound echoes, every word participates in myriad metaphors: "The rimes of this poetry are correspondences, workings of figures and patterns of figures in which we apprehend the whole we do not see" (*HD*,I.3, 67). Duncan's most intense and sustained transgressions of the real consist in the relentless metaphorizing, which, occurring inside a cave, reverberates much longer than one would like for mere communication. Metaphor can be conceived of as the seed of poetry; in Duncan's probings of the "structure of rime," the circling process of metaphorizing becomes an end in itself – as though it would push aside all other aspects of poetry. Donald Pease has noted the centrality of metaphorizing in Emerson's writing as well: "So pervasive is this metaphorizing that neither ideas nor God (Emerson's apparent 'god' terms) seems free of it. Emersonian ideas can reveal themselves only as qualities common to two objects and God himself serves only as the switch point where each 'fossil metaphor' passes into a new relation: 'In God every end is converted into new means.' In other words, Emerson's style converts even its most fundamental terms into dominant metaphors rather than ontological entities."[15] It seems as if, in the ungrounded situation of American poetry, the transitive function of metaphor that unites poetry with an agreed-upon reality has been abrogated, and our poets have entered a *mise-en-abîme* in which metaphor provides the ground for itself.

In the cases of Emerson and Duncan, the constant activity of metaphorizing makes it extremely difficult for a critic to take a detached stance from which to evaluate. One of the standard tools a critic uses to grasp the work of a writer is to examine not only the obvious figures of speech but to look at all of the language metaphorically, in order to flesh out the unsaid and thus provide a greater context for understanding the text. In the art of discovering metaphors, Emerson and Duncan have already anticipated and regulated the reader. These poets are themselves consummately skillful explorers of metaphor, who use their own metaphors in a circular fashion to enact the process of metaphoricity. In a discussion of Emerson's "transparent eyeball," for instance ("I become a transparent eyeball; I am nothing; I see all; the currents of the Universal Being circulate through me; I am part or particle of God" [*SE*, 189]), Donald Pease concludes that this metaphor is much more than a metaphor:

> If we define metaphor as that by means of which something is itself by becoming something else, the transparent eyeball, as the charged space something moves through to become something else, refers to the very activity of making metaphor, the transition of one term into another (a movement, by the way, which also makes all quests for meaning and purposes possible). Consequently, one cannot call the transparent eyeball a metaphor; it is rather the metaphorizing power, the motive power or principle upon which metaphor works. (Pease, 226)

Pease makes the same claim for the image of the circle, calling it "Emerson's metaphor for metaphoricity, for the circle is a point always differing from itself, a decentering center condemned to trace a periphery as a means of describing its content" (Pease, 294).

Duncan, too, has many ways of enacting metaphoricity. In addition to the seed-images discussed above, he has a number of privileged terms for metaphoricity that appear throughout his writing, such as rime, love, war, law, dance, field, sentence, and so on – all of which describe the site of interchange in which metaphors occur. Another way that Duncan explores metaphoricity is through his use of syntax: By writing a syntax that twists and turns, he reveals hidden metaphorical possibilities and puns in his language and that of others; his syntax forces us to see how (in the psychopathology of everyday life), by saying one thing, we are also saying another:

> In "The Structure of Rime I," it came to me in writing that "a snake-like beauty in the living changes of syntax" spoke, and cried;
>
> *Jacob wrestled with Sleep – you who fall into Nothingness and dread Sleep. He wrestled with Sleep like a man reading a strong sentence.*
>
> It has seemed to me that I wrestle with the syntax of the world of my experience to bring forward into the Day the twisted syntax of my human language that will be changed in that contest even with what I dread there. And recently I have come to think of Poetry more and more as a wrestling with Form to liberate Form. The figure of Jacob returns again and again to my thought. (*FC,* 8)

As Duncan wrestles like Jacob with syntax, his sentences turn back upon themselves, like dreams twisting free of the coils of deadly habit. Employing convoluted syntax, he fashions sentences that seem as though they were written from the dreamworld of continual metaphoricity rather than the real world of determinate fact. Under the aegis of Hermes, Duncan engages shifty grammatical devices – such as a deliberately ambiguous use of restrictive and nonrestrictive clauses, the conversion of gerunds back into verbs, the use of appositive phrases as though they were predicates, puns that can function as both nouns and verbs, and the tacking on of a verb to a predicate object in order to make the object become a subject – to keep his sentences circling, forcing them beyond the bounds of the complete statement usually staked out by the hypotactic sentence.[16] All of his characteristic syntactic abnormalities flourish in the following prose paragraph from his prose-and-verse poem "The Museum." Speaking of the work of the Muses in the architecture of the museum, Duncan writes:

> In certain designs they are most present, and in their presence I come, I realize, into their design. What I see now is a shadowd

space, a shell in time, a silent alcove in thunder, in which the
stony everlasting gaze looses itself in my coming into its plan. It
is an horizon coming in from what we cannot see to sound in
sight that is female. Moving toward an orison of the visible.
From this carving out of thought of an arrival, the figure of a
womanly grace invades the sound of the heart that beats for her,
and, in number, repeats in a run of alcoves – shadowd radiance
upon shadowd radiance – beyond the body of this Woman, the
body of these women. In the Museum – as in the labyrinth at
Knossos, the Minotaur; as in the head of the Great God, the
hawk Horus returning – a Woman that is a company of women
moves.   (*GW*, 59)

The "snake-like" suppleness and twisting quality of Duncan's prose
style appears not only in his poetry but also in his essays. Particularly
during the sixties – arguably the height of his career – when Duncan was
at work on *Roots and Branches, Bending the Bow,* and *Tribunals,* he wrote a
number of essays that contain some of his best writing. In "The Truth
and Life of Myth," "Towards an Open Universe," "Ideas of the Meaning
of Form," "Man's Fulfillment in Order and Strife," "The Sweetness and
Greatness of Dante's *Divine Comedy,*" "Changing Perspectives in Reading
Whitman," and the many chapters published from *The H. D. Book,* there
is a grandeur to the diction and rhythm of his sentences, a directness in
showing the interrelated scales of meaning in which he works, and a
supple, elastic, circular syntax that make his prose powerful and compelling in ways his poetry sometimes shies away from and sometimes over-
steps. Like the prose of other modern masters of the poetic essay, such as
Walter Benjamin, Gaston Bachelard, or Roland Barthes, Duncan's essays
exhibit the full delight and scope of writing as a world that one can
inhabit – inventing, for instance, delicate modes of evoking childhood
consciousness and of uncovering the autobiographical as an aspect of
poetics. Through these essays, and through his readings and lectures in
cities and at college campuses across the nation, Duncan became one of
the premier teachers of the power of poetry of his generation. His essays
give moving and convincing testimony to his belief in this power, and as
such have provided an impressive grounding for the poetry of his generation and those subsequent.

In their grounding function, however, Duncan's essays do not merely
testify to the power of poetry; they also make the poetry possible and, to
a certain extent, take its place. The conviction about the efficacy of poetry
that rings through them responds to the central anxiety of American
poets about whether poetry is possible under present conditions.
Through his essays, Duncan created a vast idiosyncratic tradition and a

proving ground of metaphoricity that go a long way toward repairing the lack of an originary tradition. When Duncan's best essays (or Olson's, for that matter) seem to outstrip the accomplishment of much of his poetry, we are confronting a complex phenomenon: a major poet whose verse seems to topple over sometimes for lack of sufficient grounding but whose essays provide that ground for a large number of other poets. A half-century ago, F. O. Matthiessen commented on the fact that many of the major American writers of the nineteenth century who would have been poets fell short of achieving that stature:

> Emerson, Thoreau, and Whitman all conceived of themselves primarily as poets, though, judged strictly by form, none of them was. All of them would have agreed with Emerson's decree that "it is not metres, but a metre-making argument that makes a poem"; for, with the release of energy in which they shared, they were sure that their content outran the boundaries of earlier conventions of expression. But the writing of poetry becomes inordinately difficult without a living tradition to draw upon and modify. Thoreau and Melville evolved richly modulated harmonies in their prose rhythms but were able to command far less music when they tried to borrow the more exacting medium of verse, which had hardly yet become acclimated in America.[17]

Although Matthiessen may have thought that T. S. Eliot proved once and for all that Americans are capable of borrowing "the more exacting medium of verse," I have tried to show that Eliot himself was far from immune to experiencing the inordinate difficulty of writing "without a living tradition to draw upon and modify." Like Eliot's tremendously influential essays and those of Emerson, the essays of Duncan and Olson continue to provide the support whose necessity Duncan unmistakably points to by calling his last two volumes of poetry *Ground Work*.

Stylistically, the essays of both Duncan and Olson make important contributions to the invention of American forms of writing. Like Thoreau and Melville, they "evolved richly modulated harmonies in their prose rhythms," though of different sorts from one another and from their nineteenth-century precursors. In both his investigations of other writers and in the quality of his own prose, Duncan chimes in with Emerson, who insists that poetry gains sustenance and even expression in prose:

> There are also prose poets. Thomas Taylor, the Platonist, for instance, is really a better man of imagination, a better poet, or perhaps I should say a better feeder to a poet, than any man between Milton and Wordsworth. Thomas Moore had the magna-

nimity to say, "If Burke and Bacon were not poets (measured lines not being necessary to constitute one), he did not know what poetry meant." And every good reader will easily recall expressions or passages in works of pure science which have given him the same pleasure which he seeks in professed poets.[18]

There is a good deal of equivocation about what constitutes a poet in this statement by Emerson. He begins by claiming unequivocally that there are prose poets. Thomas Taylor, also a favorite of Duncan, provides a model for such a poet, who would slip into an enviable berth right between Milton and Wordsworth. But in his claim for Taylor (and, of course, for himself, since with his prose he hopes to slip into that same berth), Emerson offers three phrases in apposition that are by no means obviously equivalent: "a better man of imagination, a better poet, or perhaps I should say a better feeder to a poet." It would be quite easy to separate these three phrases and imagine them as applying to three separate individuals; none of the three roles – man of imagination, poet, or feeder of poets – necessarily includes the other two. However, by placing them in conjunction, Emerson seeks to claim that imaginative prose and (more importantly, for our purposes) sustaining prose, such as he and Duncan engage in, perform the functions of poetry so well that they can elevate a writer into the stature of a Milton or a Wordsworth. Just as Milton and Wordsworth provided the nineteenth century with heroic images of the poet that, notwithstanding the competitive anxieties they provoked, supplied English poets with incontrovertible evidence of a tradition capable of sustaining major poetry, so Emerson sought to be a "better feeder" to American poets, and thus to earn himself a central place in the American poetic pantheon.

Emerson's anxieties about his poetic talents are well known; they were so central to his self-image that, in the earliest extant letter to his second wife, he felt it necessary to confess his poetic shortcomings and to recommend his compensatory abilities:

> I am born a poet, of a low class without doubt yet a poet. That is my nature & vocation. My singing be sure is very "husky," & is for the most part in prose. Still am I a poet in the sense of a perceiver & dear lover of the harmonies that are in the soul & in matter, & specially of the correspondences between these & those.[19]

In contrast, Robert Duncan's impediment is not an unmusical huskiness but, rather, a too persistently tinkling musicality; sometimes he appears to be so enamored of singing that he would risk being labeled by Emerson as a "jingle man," alongside Poe. Still, notwithstanding the opposing liabilities of their poetry, the prose of Duncan and Emerson shares a love of "the harmonies that are in the soul & in matter, & specially of the correspondences between these & those," which manifests itself in a circling art of wholeness.

"ERIS IN EROS"

Harmony and song do not mark every mood or every situation in life, however; recognizing this fact, Duncan's concept of rime as "an absolute scale of resemblance and disresemblance" also includes strife or correspondences between internal and external realms that are not harmonious. Some acts and feelings go beyond bounds, are so outrageous that our circling itself reaches its limits in trying to encompass them. In the Heraclitean element of fire, Duncan finds an image of wholeness in which strife threatens to move beyond all bounds. Throughout *Bending the Bow*, written during the Vietnam War, the image of fire recurs, both as an emblem of war and as a sign of a political rage that transgresses Duncan's own self-encirclement. In "The Fire, Passages 13," the poet's meditation on Piero di Cosimo's painting *A Forest Fire* fleshes out an imagining of a forest consumed by napalm; from the di Cosimo painting Duncan associates to a contemporaneous Bosch depiction of hell, in which he imagines the visages of leaders and scientists from our own time:

> Satan looks forth from
> men's faces:
> Eisenhower's idiot grin, Nixon's
> black jaw, the sly glare in Goldwater's eye, or
> the look of Stevenson lying in the U.N. that our
> Nation save face •
>
> His face multiplies from the time of Roosevelt, Stalin,
> Churchill, Hitler, Mussolini;   from the dream
> of Oppenheimer, Fermi, Teller, Vannevar Bush,
>
> brooding the nightmare formulae – to win the war! the
>
> inevitable • at Los Alamos
>
> plotting the holocaust of Hiroshima •
>
> Teller openly for the Anti-Christ
>
> • glints of the evil that one sees in the power of this world
>
> (*BB*, 43–4)

Fire as an image of rage, madness, war, and evil circles through other poems in *Bending the Bow*, becoming particularly intense in Duncan's most virulently antiwar poems, "Up Rising, Passages 25" and "The Soldiers, Passages 26." The fire of greed and destruction that rages out of control metamorphoses in both of these poems, and in "The Multiversity, Passages 21" and "Moira's Cathedral," into a monstrous hydra, whose heads are shown (in "The Multiversity") to be the military-industrial-educational complex. In "Moira's Cathedral" Duncan depicts evil as a hydra with limitless heads, whose very being resists all boundaries:

MOIRA'S CATHEDRAL

"The imaginary numbers," wrote Gottfried Wilhelm
von Leibnitz in 1702, "are a wonderful flight of God's Spirit;
they are almost an amphibian between being and not being."

A field is "orderd" if the sizes of its
elements can be compared.

The sizes of its elements cannot
be compared.   For in the Eye of the Creator

the trembling of a leaf
in the roar of gun-fire,

the fall of a tree,   strikes dismay.

A thousand men go into the dirt and flood to die
having nor name nor proportion
in their numbers.   We

lose count.   An army—

a single man rising
rememberd   falling back
—I do not know who he is—
—where he is—

cries out.

Is it $17 million a day, a
million men finally to be laid down
in wager?

There is no Limit.

The hydra breaks from his confines
into Day's palaces

as many heads as he wants

(he moves the living bodies of men
    forward
    to fill the gap •)

      to win.   Destroying

fields of rice, villages, bridges,
    factories, defenses . . .

At the Grand Poker Table,
burning heads of their stogies
    illustrating the battlefields,

eyes of that entity   counting

      on the play

    his hands

shuffling the cards, beyond number.
          (*BB,* 95–6)

These poems of moral outrage, which speak of an evil beyond limit, beyond number, beyond measure, take Duncan to the very limits of a poetry of wholeness, for when the poet begins to speak against the other, enforcing separation, division, and ostracism of that which he conceives of as evil, then the circle breaks apart. In the lecture "Man's Fulfillment in Order and Strife," Duncan gives a detailed gloss on the poem "Up Rising," insisting that no matter how close it comes to demagoguery in its name-calling and denunciation of evil, it still maintains a sense of responsibility and repentance for the very acts it denounces:

> It would be easier if our fears were not identical with our hopes, and clearer if the forces of evil – of whatever would bind us against our will – which we see men give themselves over to could be disowned. To disown them from our own character, from the decisive stamp we created as our immediate "self" in being, we are resolved, in so far as we would contribute to the good; but we cannot disown these evils from the fate of Man in which as men we share. We must acknowledge how deeply the intent of the whole is dramatic, and where we would see further than our own sense of what is good to the goods of our history at large, we find them worked in darks as well as lights. . . . (*FC,* 139)

In his refusal to be bound by the walls of an individual identity, Duncan reclaims the whole by seeing his responsibility as an American and as a human being for the suffering he abhors. Although we must disown evil "from our own character," we cannot blot out the necessary interplay of good and evil, of dark and light, in the unfathomable course of history. And if we cannot, he asserts, accept that very evil as in some at least imaginative way ours, we block ourselves from a recognition of the fullness of our humanity.

Another way in which Duncan invites the fiery, the outrageous, back within the boundaries of the whole is by reinscribing the evil within a larger sense of narrative, recognizing that "the intent of the whole is dramatic," that history itself is (contra Olson) an enactment. For Duncan, the story is always mythical and, as such, allied with the worlds of dream and childhood. "The Fire," from which we quoted above, is reinscribed by childhood in this way, beginning and ending with a matrix of single words without syntax, which, taken together, suggest a cool, watery, prelapsarian world. In a commentary on this poem, Duncan points out the deliberate contrast between the framing "ideogram of a childhood memory," which occurs in the first and last lines of the poem, and the prophetic denunciation that it encloses:

> When, in the poem "The Fire," Bosch's Christ, out of the hell of the seventeenth-century religious wars into the hell of our own century's wars between Capitalist and Communist, appeared . . . surrounded by the faces of the contemporary public men of our Permanent War Economy, the very faces Bosch painted, leering or piously grimacing, protesting their love of order as they preside over the violation of Asia, these were earlier faces I had seen, long before I saw Bosch. Bosch's painting was a rime. And against their evil, the ever-returning scene of brutality and will, I raised a scene of early childhood, a dawn-of-man scene, with its play of leaf-boats and sand harbors in a mountain stream, close and cool with shadow and sunlight, that barely holds. Moments of childhood are created as Edens, the mythic seed of a power in the story to come. (FC, 32–3)

In childhood we first learn the myths, which, says Duncan, are actually the truths of wholeness by which our lives will make sense. In his central meditation upon the relation of myth to a poetics of circling, "The Truth and Life of Myth" (FC, 1–59), he states that "for the poet the common property of man's myths is a resource of working material, a grammar of rimes" (FC, 18). We learn these myths as bedtime stories, so that when they begin to enact themselves in our lives, we will recognize intuitively the stories to which we belong. The traditional content of myths is so potent – it so threatens the orders we construct for making our lives safe (our reality) – that we must learn myths when we are at our most innocent and least likely to be alarmed by the continual transgression of boundaries occurring in them: "It is important here that the myth be first so familiar, so much no-more-than an old story, that the poet is at home with what is most perilous" (*FC,* 18).

Duncan's "Passages" sequence reinscribes contemporary scenes of evil, monstrosity, and outrage into mythical scenarios, illustrating that fire, even though it reaches the unconscionable heights of a holocaust, is still a natural element. Although in the following passage from "The Poet" Emerson makes it sound easy when he, too, speaks of the poet as naturalizing the outrageous through an art of wholeness, he is characterizing the ideal American poet, of whom he later says, "I look in vain for the poet whom I describe" (*RWE,* 324):

> For, as it is dislocation and detachment from the life of God, that makes things ugly, the poet, who reattaches things to nature and the Whole, – reattaching even artificial things, and violations of nature, to nature, by a deeper insight – disposes very easily of the most disagreeable facts. Readers of poetry see the factory village and the railway, and fancy that the poetry of the landscape is broken up by these; for these works of art are not yet consecrated in their reading; but the poet sees them fall within the great Order not less than the beehive, or the spider's geometrical web. Nature adopts them very fast into her vital circles, and the gliding train of cars she loves like her own. (*RWE,* 314–15)

Duncan follows assiduously the Emersonian prescription for reattaching "artificial" things to the whole.[20] Whereas Emerson sees the whole most powerfully manifest in nature, Duncan finds it in myths; just as Emerson reads nature as a hieroglyphic language through which the spirit speaks ("the world is a temple, whose walls are covered with emblems, pictures, and commandments of the Deity" ["The Poet," *RWE,* 314]), so Duncan finds his oracle in myths: "I was already a convert to the Romantic spirit, and myth in that spirit is not only a story that expresses the soul but a story that awakens the soul to the real persons of its romance, in which the actual and the spiritual are revealed, one in the other" (*FC,* 31).

The myths that Duncan uses to encompass the greatest diversity of feelings, experiences, researches, and imaginings are stories of love, particularly those told about Eros and Christ. Duncan works with the Hesiodic, Homeric, and Orphic myths of Eros, but his favorite is Apuleius's "Cupid and Psyche" from *The Golden Ass.* His myths of Christ are sometimes taken from scripture, but more often they come from less orthodox sources like gnosticism, hermeticism and the occult, the Moravian "Love Feast," and the visions of poets, artists, and saints. For Duncan, love is the deepest experience of the circling art. If we can say that for Olson the secret that animates poetry and life is the truth of self-identity, then for Duncan we would want to say that the equivalent secret is love.[21]

In love he finds what makes possible his poetic vocation: permission, participation in greater and greater circles of life, the acceptance of difference, the loosing of restrictive bonds, and the basis (as in Whitman) of a true politics of commonality. And through love he encircles within his poetry the most seemingly incommensurate experiences of strife, adversity, and inarticulateness. One of Duncan's favorite puns, Eros/Eris (Love/Strife), encapsulates the paradoxical quality of the wholeness he associates with love; the riming of these contrary states is never far from any whole that Duncan constructs: without strife, he asks – without anger, grief, despair, sickness, death – how can love be true? In the following poem, he acknowledges not just the conjunction of Eros and Eris but also that of dumbness and speech, finding the ground of his life in love to have been mysteriously articulated in a moment of strife during which he could not speak:

SUCH IS THE SICKNESS OF MANY A GOOD THING

Was he then Adam of the Burning Way?
hid away in the heat like wrath
conceald in Love's face,
or the seed, Eris in Eros,
key and lock
of what I was?   I could not speak
the releasing
word.   For into a dark
matter he came
and askt me to say what
I could not say.   "I . ."

All the flame in me stopt
against my tongue.
My heart was a stone, a dumb
unmanageable thing in me,
a darkness that stood athwart
his need
for the enlightening, the
"I love you" that has
only this one quick in time,
this one start
when its moment is true.

Such is the sickness of many a good thing
that now into my life from long ago this
refusing to say I love you has bound

> the weeping, the yielding, the
>> yearning to be taken again,
> into a knot, a waiting, a string
>
> so taut it taunts the song,
> it resists the touch. It grows dark
> to draw down the lover's hand
> from its lightness to what's
>> underground.   (BB, 6)

Like a Hermes who cannot deliver his message but must nonetheless function as guide to the underworld, Duncan leads the lover underground to a love in death, an Eros in the dark (whom Psyche should accept, but foolishly wishes to understand), which all of Duncan's love poetry strives to articulate, a primal ground of love that is most properly conveyed in tones of yearning, anguish, and grief – for both the unfulfillable nature of the circle of love and for its inexpressible darkness. In the moving refrain from "Passages 36," Duncan seems to have touched the core of his experience of love, with its dual character of release and grief that creates a whole through the negative space of death:

> *Let it go. Let it go.*
> *Grief's its proper mode.*
>
> *But O,   How deep it's got to reach,*
>> *How high and wide*
>> *it's got to grow,*
> *Before it come to sufficient grief . . .*
>> (GW, 80)

* * * *

How do these experiences of grief and of dumbness in love reflect a relationship to the ground? For Duncan, his constant awareness of the cooperation of love and strife enforces a remembrance of the dark, shadowy, inexpressible truths guarded by tradition. He actively cultivates such remembrance as an antidote to the forgetfulness that can ensue when tradition is felt to be wholly given.[22] Remembrance – not as recuperation but as awareness of the dark – is a central aspect of the groundwork of circling. Duncan invokes the power of memory, Mnemosyne, the Mother of the Muses, as the goddess overseeing the "Passages" sequence in "Tribal Memories, Passages 1":

> Mnemosyne, they named her, the
>> Mother with the whispering
> featherd wings.   Memory,

the great speckled bird who broods over the
nest of souls, and her egg,
the dream in which all things are living,
I return to, leaving my self.   (*BB*, 10)

In the same poem, Duncan addresses this mothering memory as "Her-Without-Bounds," taking this appellation from one of the two passages from the Emperor Julian's *Hymn to the Mother of the Gods* that appear as an epigraph to the entire "Passages" sequence: "For the even is bounded, but the uneven is without bounds and there is no way through or out of it" (*BB*, 9). In these figures for memory as a mother, Duncan encapsulates the circling functions of wholeness and transgression as qualities of a primal ground, speaking in later "Passages" of "Story, Herself a mother of sorts" (*BB*, 67) and of the "Grand Mother of Images,   matrix / genetrix" (*BB*, 75), which he also identifies with the moon, "turning my poet's mind in tides of / solitude, seductive reveries, fears, resolves, outrage" (*BB*, 75). Discussing the epigraphs from the Emperor Julian, Duncan underscores the importance of memory for the form of the "Passages" sequence:

> These two passages stand as inscriptions to the entry which Passages 1 is upon a series having no beginning and no end as its condition of form. The sequence we hear belongs to a field in which we know there is no consequence. In the true form of the poem all its parts co-operate, co-exist. What we hear at last has long preceded what remains of what first we heard. It is our own Memory-field as we listen in which the truth of that form is created, in which, as we comprehend the form, all its parts are present in one fabric. We wove strand after strand, line after line; but for those who at last see the cloth there is no first strand or second strand; the design does not begin in a certain place but where the admirer's eye chooses to begin in seeing.[23]

The circling memory that informs Duncan's sense of form is identified most powerfully by the poet with the earth, which becomes the "field" for his projectivist poetry. In an essay on *The Opening of the Field*, Michael Davidson discusses the derivation and ramifications of the field image in that book. Davidson quotes from an unpublished preface, in which Duncan says, "In this book I take the field as a theme or rather reference point; it is the field which appeared in my earliest remembered childhood dream where children danced and an omen came of blowing grass where no wind was and a king of the game was chosen, followed by terror, deluge, by what I do not remember."[24] Duncan's biological mother died during his birth, and this "Atlantis" dream, as he calls it, he also reads as a birth-trauma dream, a memory of the loss of the mother (*HD*, I.5, 18). Throughout *The Opening of the Field*, Davidson points out, images from this dream recur, repeated also in the children dancing on both the front cover and the title page of the Grove Press edition. With the loss of the biological mother there is also a loss of connection to the ground, so that the cataclysmic dream enacts, through both horror and memory, the loss of the ground and the repeated attempts to find it again. In "Often I am permitted to Return to a Meadow," the inaugural poem of the book, the fictive field ("a scene made-up by the mind") opens into the dream meadow ("an eternal pasture folded in all thought"), which is presided over by the mother of memory and articulation: "She it is Queen Under the Hill / whose hosts are a disturbance of words within words / that is a field folded" (*OF*, 7). The hosts of memory and language, of remembered dumbness within articulation, are also figured as the children from Duncan's dream, who perform a circle dance on the meadow:

> On the hill before the wind came
> the grass moved toward the one sea,
> blade after blade dancing in waves.
>
> There the children turn the ring to the left.
> There the children turn the ring to the right.
> Dancing . . . Dancing . . .
>
> And the lonely psyche goes up thru the boy to the king
> that in the caves of history dreams.
> Round and round the children turn.
> London Bridge that is a kingdom falls.   (*OF*, 68)

The poem from which this passage is taken, "A Poem Beginning with a Line by Pindar," forms the centerpiece of *The Opening of the Field*, not only by linking many major themes in Duncan's work, but also by discovering an original projectivist form that brings Duncan fully into the practice of the Black Mountain community. The themes of the poem include the myths of Hermes, Jason, and Cupid and Psyche; the cooperation of strife with love ("Fate, spinning, / knots the threads for Love. / / Jealousy, ignorance, the hurt . . . serve them" [*OF*, 63; ellipsis Duncan's]); the modern American betrayal of the lover's democracy imagined by Whitman; an invocation of the proud but broken tutelary spirits of Pound and Williams; poetic meditations upon particular paintings; "the boundary walker" who "renders clear / the days of a life from the surrounding medium" (*OF*, 67); the creative misreading of prior texts (in this case a Pindaric ode); and "the willful children / / clockwise and counter-clockwise turning" (*OF*, 69). But more important than this collocation of themes was Duncan's discovery in this poem of a poetics of recognition that made possible much of his later poetry, including the "Passages" sequence, which is his most ambitious work. In "The Truth and Life of Myth," Duncan describes the creative mistake that released him into the remarkable series of projectivist recognitions that comprise this eight-page poem:

> When in the inception of "A Poem Beginning with a Line by Pindar," reading late at night the third line of the first Pythian Ode in the translation by Wade-Gery and Bowra, my mind lost hold of Pindar's sense and was faced with certain puns, so that the words *light, foot, hears, you, brightness, begins* moved in a world beyond my reading, these were no longer words alone but also powers in a theogony, having resonances in Hesiodic and Orphic cosmogonies where the foot that moves in the dance of the poem appears as the pulse of measures in first things. Immediately, sight of Goya's great canvas [*Cupid and Psyche*], once seen in the Marquis de Cambo's collection in Barcelona, came to me, like a wave, carrying the vision – out of the evocation of the fragment from Pindar and out of Goya's pictorial evocation to add their masterly powers to my own – the living vision, Cupid and Psyche, were there . . . but in the power of those first Words – Light, Foot, Hears, You, Brightness, Begins – He was the primal Eros, and she, the First Soul. Waking into the reality of the poem, so that the room where I wrote, the fact that I was writing, and the catalytic process of the works of art, passed into the process of the poem itself, dimly underlying the work, as in actual life we may be aware that dream processes are at work, the poem as I wrote forming such a powerful nexus or vehicle of this transcendent reality of Eros and Psyche and of the revelations flowing out of the myth they belonged to, I was hard pressed to keep up with the formations as they came. (*FC*, 17)

In this account, Duncan describes the "disturbance of words within words," which he also calls "a field folded," and ascribes it to the mother of memory (*OF*, 7). On the border of the dream state, in the realm of not-understanding, the poet's reading is disturbed by puns, whose charge comes from their association with memories – both of personal experiences and of texts and paintings. Once he is, as it were, permitted to return to this meadow of charged resonances, the recognitions begin to occur so rapidly that, he reports, "I was hard pressed to keep up with the formations as they came." Duncan always describes this perception of interlocking recognitions as a sense of "fit," occurring within "the structure of rime," which simultaneously completes a whole and crosses a boundary: "The part in its fitting does not lock but unlocks; what was

closed is opend" (*BB*, iv). In this heightened moment of loosened attention, the poet feels guided by particular words into the secret realm of
power, which includes even the powers informing other works of art.
Learning to listen to language in such a way as to provoke this striking
series of recognitions is an extremely difficult accomplishment – one that
Duncan rightly celebrates as occurring with the Pindar poem and as
initiating his later poetry. Although recognitions are a constant aspect of
the work of understanding – we are always sensing the way things fit into
a pattern or a whole – Olson emphasizes an obedience to the instantaneous quality of a chain of recognitions as a primary duty of the
projectivist poet ("ONE PERCEPTION MUST IMMEDIATELY AND DIRECTLY
LEAD TO A FURTHER PERCEPTION" [*SW*, 17]); for the opening of one recognition into the next creates the swiftly expanding sense of rime that is, for
Duncan, the central poetic experience. As Duncan applied to the "Passages" sequence the projectivist sense of recognition he discovered in the
"Pindar" poem, Olson began to admit that Duncan was fulfilling the
largest terms for poetry that Olson himself had imagined: "Unbeliev-
able, these new *Passages*. . . . I mean he's moved into a – almost a status
or something, if I may use that word – a condition of status. I don't mean
stasis, I mean literally STATUS. He's become a BIG poet, like Yeats" (*Muth*
II, 72).

Through this projectivist art of circling, Duncan achieves "status" –
standing – a place from which to write. By means of his twin convictions
that harmony, or the sense of fit, runs throughout the universe at every
level, and that the poet apprehends such correspondences through instantaneous recognitions bestowed by the dream-mother of memory, he
creates a poetry and a world of ever-expanding rime as a groundwork for
his writing. If tradition cannot supply him with a world of underwritten
meanings, then he can use his circling abilities to construct a web of
correspondences densely woven enough that he can stand upon it. Sometimes, one feels that Duncan becomes obsessive in his reiterated rimes, a
quality indicative of the extensive anxiety about groundlessness that his
circling art is meant to allay. For instance, in his desire to assure himself
of an "absolute scale of resemblance and disresemblance," he looks to the
occult, not just for its associations to his childhood, but also because it
carries the process of metaphorical resemblance much farther than does
orthodox religion or empirical science.

In the occult imagination there is an image of Jacob's ladder, of rungs
of corresponding levels to the world, which Duncan uses to invoke the
interlocking fit of a riming reality:

> In the great figure of many figures the four
> directions and empires

> change into four times, and opposites of
>   opposites meet and mate,
> separating and joining, ascending a ladder of litanies
>   until they are "sent" –
> losing themselves in each other's being
>   found again.   (*BB*, 118)

The ladder goes both up and down (Heraclitus: "The same road goes both up and down.");[25] or as Duncan puts it, invoking the sexual "underworld" as a power that "sends" us climbing down to an initiation: "This way below is the way above, / the mouth of the cave or temple growing moist / shining, to allow the neophyte / full entrance" (*BB* 6). In its broadest sense, the "ladder of litanies" that Duncan goes up and down consists of the following steps: self, household, city, nation, earth, cosmos. In one of his many assertions of affinity between different steps of the ladder, Duncan says, "The imagination of the cosmos is as immediate to me as the imagination of my household or my self, for I have taken my being in what I know of the sun and of the magnitude of the cosmos, as I have taken my being in what I know of domestic things" (*FC*, 76). Each of the steps on this ladder, or any of the others Duncan constructs, can be conceived of as a circle; "Passages" investigates the metaphorical passage between these circles.

Every rung of the ladder, of course, comprises a circle that can always be circumscribed by a further circle, so that the circles themselves whirl in a circling dance – as in the square dance of opposites that produces the "ladder of litanies" in the passage quoted above. Duncan invokes this grand circle dance many times in his poetry, memorably, for instance, in a late love poem, "Circulations of the Song" (*GW*, 165–75), dedicated to and drawing upon the poet Rumi, who founded the Sufi order of whirling dervishes. At the core of the experience of the dervish dance there is a great silence and stillness, whose strangeness Duncan, too, finds central to his poetic art of circling; although seeming to whirl in every direction, looking down every avenue conceivable for his inspiration, the poet of wholeness must learn to wait and be quiet. "We all stand waiting, empty," says Emerson, "– knowing, possibly, that we can be full," waiting for the grace of the god who transforms facts into metaphors and sets them all to dancing. In our daily lives we are like frozen statues,

> surrounded by mighty symbols which are not symbols to us, but prose and trivial toys. Then cometh the god, and converts the statues into fiery men, and by a flash of his eye burns up the veil which shrouded all things, and the meaning of the very furniture, of cup and saucer, of chair and clock and tester, is manifest. The facts which loomed so large in the fogs of yesterday, – property,

climate, breeding, personal beauty, and the like, have strangely changed their proportions. All that we reckoned settled shakes and rattles; and literatures, cities, climates, religions, leave their foundations, and dance before our eyes. And yet here again see the swift circumspection! Good as is discourse, silence is better, and shames it. ("Circles," *RWE*, 300–1)

Since American poetry cannot pretend to a permanent ground, then maybe we would do better to embrace the fact that our condition is more like a permanent earthquake. If while the earthquake "shakes and rattles" we take refuge in that strange silence, then we might be able to see the earthquake as a dance and take up its measure. This is what the circling art of wholeness proposes to do: watch the firm foundation shake loose and join it in the dance. In a poem from *The Opening of the Field*, Duncan captures in the image of the dance most of the senses of circling we have explored in this chapter, returning finally to "the silent danceground":

THE DANCE

from its dancers circulates among the other
        dancers. This
would–have–been feverish cool excess of
        movement makes
each man   hit the pitch   co-
        ordinate.

Lovely their feet pound the green solid meadow.
        The dancers
mimic flowers—root stem stamen and petal
        our words are,
our articulations,   our
        measures.

It is the joy that exceeds pleasure.

    You have passd the count, she said

or I understood from her eyes. Now
old Friedl has grown so lovely in my years,

    I remember only the truth.
    I swear by my yearning.

    You have conquerd the yearning, she said
    The numbers have enterd your feet

        turn   turn   turn

When you're real gone, boy, sweet boy . .

Where have I gone, Beloved?

Into the Waltz, Dancer.

Lovely our circulations sweeten the meadow.
In Rubens' riotous scene the May dancers teach us our learning
  seeks abandon!

Maximus calld us to dance the Man.
We calld *him*   to call
    season   out of season–

d mind!
              Lovely
join we to dance green to the meadow.

Whitman was right.   Our names are left
      like leaves of grass,
likeness and liking,   the human greenness

tough as grass that survives cruelest seasons.

> I see now a radiance.
> The dancers are gone.
> They lie in heaps, exhausted,
> dead tired we say.
> They'll sleep until noon.

> But I returned early
> for the silence,
> for the lovely pang that is
> a flower,
> returnd to the silent dance-ground.

(That was my job that summer. I'd dance until three, then up to get
the hall swept before nine – beer bottles, cigarette butts, paper
mementos of the night before. Writing it down now, it is the after-
math, the silence, I remember, part of the dance too, an articulation
of the time of dancing . . like the almost dead sleeping is a step. I've
got it in a poem, about Friedl, moaning in the depths of. But that
was another room that summer. Part of my description. What I see
is a meadow . .

I'll slip away before they're up . .

      and see the dew shining.   (*OF*, 8–9)

Chapter 6

CONCLUSION

ENDLESSLY ROCKING: CREELEY AND WHITMAN ON REPETITION

I would like to make one more brief pairing of a projectivist poet with a transcendentalist, placing Robert Creeley's later writing against the background of Walt Whitman's "Out of the Cradle Endlessly Rocking," in order to highlight a further method of approaching the ground, and then I would like to close with some general observations about modes of grounding in American poetry. Like the previous pairings of Olson with Thoreau and Duncan with Emerson, the pairing of Creeley and Whitman does not depend upon stylistic influence but upon an underlying similarity of approach to the condition of groundlessness. In the introduction to his edition of Whitman's poems in the "Poet to Poet" series, Creeley confessed, "My own senses of Whitman were curiously numb until I was thirty."[1] In other words, he did not begin to study Whitman until after he was an established member of the Black Mountain community. And not until he entered the second phase of his poetry with the publication of *Pieces* (1969) did Creeley engage fully the method – repetition – that he shares with Whitman. Finding Whitman late, Creeley came to regard him as a major precursor to projectivist poetry. In his introduction, Creeley tells how his lack of appreciation was a result of his schooling in a modernism that obscured the Emersonian lineage. By 1972, though, he found his own grounding procedures directly affirmed by Whitman: "The constantly recurring structures in Whitman's writing, the insistently parallel sounds and rhythms, recall the patterns of the waves as I now see them daily. How can I point to *this* wave, or *that* one, and announce that it is *the* one? Rather, Whitman's method seems to me a process of sometimes endless gathering, moving in the energy of his own attention and impulse" (*Whitman*, 15).

"Moving in the energy of his own attention and impulse," the later Creeley shares with Whitman a method of confronting groundlessness by the "sometimes endless gathering" activities of repetition and return. As Whitman finds, though, when he returns to the Long Island seashore of his childhood in "Out of the Cradle Endlessly Rocking," the return is always to a new place, and the repetition, as Creeley points out, is always a gathering. In "The Descent," William Carlos Williams likewise invokes the process of repetition, which he ascribes to memory:

> Memory is a kind
> of accomplishment
> a sort of renewal
> even
> an initiation, since the spaces it opens are new places
> inhabited by hordes
> heretofore unrealized[2]

Here, the reiterative quality of memory takes precedence over the allied but somewhat different emphasis on memory as a circling activity of wholeness in Duncan's poetics. Although Williams clearly understands the regenerative power of repetition, he, too, does not practice repetition-that-gathers as a central poetic method in the way that Creeley, Whitman, and also Gertrude Stein do. For Creeley and Whitman, in particular, repetition involves a return to what we usually consider the background of our lives – that *from* which rather than *to* which we attend – such as the body, memory, mother, death, and the ocean; the background does not come forward as a subject but is invoked as an informing presence through repetition.

We might coin the term "backgrounding" to cover this concerted attempt to invoke unpresentable preconditions, contrasting it with the more familiar critical term "foregrounding." While foregrounding brings forward into our awareness elements (primarily linguistic) that we usually ignore, backgrounding relegates the subject matter of a poem to a secondary position by presenting the act of grounding itself. In foregrounding, as in collage, a piece of unacknowledged or unvalued reality is lifted from its context and brought into the spotlight; backgrounding, however, as in the silences of John Cage's music and poetry, draws our attention to the indivisible background, asking us to value it as much as, or more, than the objects under the spotlight. Creeley and Whitman use backgrounding to invoke a ground by pointing at the existential components of particular lived moments, exploring the background senses of "here" and "now" (to use two of Creeley's favorite terms) in which the events of our lives occur.

When the bard of Whitman's "Out of the Cradle Endlessly Rocking" returns to the seashore of his childhood, his motive seems, not a retro-spective one of commemorating the annunciation of his vocation, but rather a present need to interrogate further the ground upon which he writes. Remembering the song of the forlorn mockingbird, the bard realizes that the earlier awakening within him of the corresponding "cries of unsatisfied love" (l. 153), while foundational for his vocation as poet, has not fully revealed its own conditions. Driven to probe deeper "the sweet hell within, / the unknown want, the destiny of me" (ll. 156–7), he now finds his lack of awareness of the grounds of writing intolerable. So he returns to "Paumanok" to inquire upon what all this desire and anguish and singing rest: "O give me the clew! (it lurks in the night here some-where,) / O if I am to have so much, let me have more!" (ll. 158–9), he begs. The ocean seems to respond to his call by enunciating in its re-iterative waves "the low and delicious word death, / And again death, death, death, death" (ll. 168–9). In closing the poem, the bard acknowl-edges that this "clew" has been offered through maternal auspices, calling it,

> . . . the key, the word up from the waves
> The word of the sweetest song and all songs,
> That strong and delicious word which, creeping to my feet,
> (Or like some old crone rocking the cradle, swathed in sweet
>   garments, bending aside,)
> The sea whispered me.   (ll. 179–83)

Probing the background of his poetic vocation, Whitman returns to his annunciation site to re-peat (ask again) his foundational question, in order, it seems, to receive a fuller affirmation of his calling. But this is not the only instance of repetition in the poem, for the answer to his re-petition comes in the repetitive waves of the sea. The poet's initial re-petitive act – asking for a reaffirmation of his calling – plunges him into a primary experience of repetition itself, which includes within it, as the passage above makes clear, the opposed qualities of death and nurturing birth. Who is the old crone rocking the cradle of poetry, who both nurtures it at its birth and promises to annihilate its very existence? Is it not tradition itself, in its background work of giving and withholding? At the end of his search for renewed justification for his poetry, Whitman finds the welcoming and warning figure, whose only act of reassurance is to repeat endlessly its welcome admonishment: you have been given everything you need to build a life of poetry, and all that you have received is shot through with death. Seeking the background for his poetry, Whitman locates it in death, a condition absolutely devoid of qualities or even of awareness; this background retreats so precipitously from one's grasp that the only way to acknowledge it is by constantly repeating its name: "Death, death, death, death, death." Death is the name of that which tradition withholds. At a formal level, the poem enacts the search for tradition through its stately meters and such resoundingly traditional themes and images as love, longing, death, the moon, the birds, the ocean, and the crone; as Whitman himself claimed, however, "The piece will bear reading many times – perhaps, indeed only comes forth, as from recesses, by many repetitions" (*LG, 247*).

In its repetitive investigation of many of the same themes and images, Creeley's poetry of the last two decades has taken a turn toward the background that seems to puzzle some of the readers who professed enthusiasm for his earlier writing. Dating from the breakthrough book *Pieces* (1969), Creeley's poetry and prose have undergone a transformation from the tight, sarcastic, tortured expression of a lyric or narrative moment in *For Love* (1962) and *The Gold Diggers* (1965) to a more relaxed, open-ended meditation. From the representation of a wounded ego, with its prominent pain, anger, and supplication, Creeley shifts dramatically to an exploration of the ground of experience, in which repetition plays a central part. This more expanded focus works against our habits of attention – which may account for his finding some readers inattentive. Creeley's writing asks the reader to make a basic perceptual shift, moving off from the "figure" in our mental gestalt in order to approach the ground. Unchanged by this shift in focus, though, is Creeley's characteristic intensity. Although the dramatic effect produced by searing rage or aching self-doubt in the early writing has nearly disappeared in later works like *Hello* (1978) and *Presences* (1976), the emotional intensity of the earlier work gives way to a correspondingly powerful investigation of language and appearances. Instead of pursuing the lyric poet's goal of lifting an isolate moment out of the flux and rendering it essential and timeless, Creeley patiently returns us to the ground of our experience through careful attention to the emergence of momentary appearances¹ in the mundane world. Likewise, instead of presenting his language as a newly minted vehicle for particular images or states of mind, he often gives us the simplest diction or even language overheard – whether in songs, radio, conversation, other texts, or the voice inside one's head – that provides the mental context in which we all live. A poem with an unremarkable surface, "This World," from *Later* (1979), will provide a useful example of Creeley's repetitive approach to the ground through simple words and appearances:

THIS WORLD

If night's the harder,
closer time, days

come. The morning
opens with light

at the window.
Then, as now, sun
climbs in blue sky.
At noon

on the beach
I could watch
these glittering
waves forever,

follow their sound
deep into mind
and echoes—
let light

as air
be relief.
The wind
pulls at face

and hands,
grows cold. What
can one think—
the beach

is myriad stone.
Clouds pass,
grey undersides,
white clusters

of air, all
air. Water
moves at the edges,
blue, green,

white twists
of foam.
What then
will be lost,

recovered.
What
matters as one
in this world?[3]

This poem begins in simplicity by pondering the differences between night and day as background conditions. At night the ground seems to recede, leaving one, if awake, framed in the bright, harsh light of self-reflexive attention. In the daytime one can relax this self-absorption and surrender to what the day brings (through its sexual connotation the word "come" always carries for Creeley an association to letting go or surrender). "The morning / opens with light," bringing a light to live by other than the high-intensity lamp of the relentlessly analytical mind; and this natural light of morning "opens" one (to read the verb more transitively), if one lets it, through making apparent the "window" of awareness that connects the inside with the outside. Insisting upon the repetitive quality of this shift in awareness from "night" to "day," Creeley invokes a "then" to compare to the "now" in which the sun rises once again.

Once we reach the word *now*, however, the poem seems to shift location from the self-absorbed mind caught in reflection to a present moment of engagement with the world. The sun, ruler of the temporal world, claims its place in the sky and carries the speaker with it into the fully lighted world, the world of "noon," in which the ground is called forth with particular urgency. (It is worth commenting, parenthetically, upon the subtle modulation of sound Creeley works in this poem with the simplest words. In lines three through eight, in which the sun comes to dominate the poem, Creeley orchestrates the nasal hum of *n* and *m* and the vocalic shadings of *o* and *u*. The complex rhyming of the words *morning, open, window, then, now, sun* and *moon* reinforces the repetitive though inexorable power of the sun as light of the world.) The speaker is located now on the beach, in that open, relaxed posture in which the empty mind takes interest in what is happening around it. In the statement, "I could watch / these glittering / waves forever," the speaker uses the conditional tense, offering himself provisionally to the sun and the reiterative context it illumines. As the speaker follows through on this impulse of self-offering, he progressively relinquishes the constant search by the restless mind for something of "interest." Instead, the background phenomenon of unfixable waves comes to control his awareness, as though their rhythmic reverberations dominate the senses and take over the mind – controlling not only its present focus but also arranging its latent contents through penetrant "echoes." Once the grounding activity of the waves affects this reorganization of consciousness, the speaker becomes aware of the even more subtle principle that illumines the ground itself: if he can "let light / as air / be relief," then he can, in the insistent alliteration and assonance of those lines, call forth an illuminative secret from the sun that, in its palpable but unfathomable identification with the ground, corresponds uncannily tc the illuminative secret of death that Whitman called forth from the waves.

Like "Out of the Cradle," "This World" addresses questions to the ground. However, rather than coming to the scene, as Whitman does, primed with questions, Creeley finds questions arising from the words and appearances that occur in the poem; but the answers, as in Whitman's poem, come in the form of a return to the actual context rather than in an intellectual proposition. For instance, after the relief of feeling "light" //as air," the air takes motion as wind and begins to "pull at face / and hands" – to awaken the expressive and manipulative parts of the body – causing the speaker to shrink back and feel cold. At this point the mind returns to action, asking its own constitutive question: "What / can one think." Instead of responding with personal preoccupations, such as were likely predominant during the "harder / closer" night, the speaker looks to the background for an answer: "the beach," he finds, "is myriad stone." This "myriad stone" may seem a cold, mute reply to the inquiring mind, but its very resistance and unassimilability are oddly appropriate, like the withholding quality of tradition. Creeley hopes to rest upon the "myriad stone," much as Whitman claims granite for his grounding in "Song of Myself": "My foothold is tenon'd and mortis'd in granite" (LG, 48).

In the next three stanzas of "This World," the speaker immerses himself in the streaming context – clouds, air, water – and is content with whatever arises from it, such as "white twists / of foam." At the end of the poem, the pondering mind comes back for three final questions:

> What then
> will be lost,
>
> recovered.
> What
> matters as one
> in this world?

These are the sorts of questions Creeley asks with increasing frequency in his later poetry and prose, where the relationship of the individual identity to the ground becomes paramount. The aging man, aware of the passage of time, asks who he is and to what extent he can be said to live in his body, in his memory, in his actions. By repeating these nagging questions at the end of a poem in which primacy has been accorded throughout to the ground rather than the mind, Creeley appears to be surrendering such questions to the context – as though the silent ground were given the last word.

However, before he surrenders to silence in the last sentence of the poem, Creeley places a marked insistence on the word *one,* which could mean, in context, oneself, integrity, singularity, or even some kind of unity. *One* is the central pun in his vocabulary; it is both a pronoun (which seems to fluctuate, in our usage, between first and third persons) and a number, suggesting a conglomeration of meanings: a self that is both subjective and distanced; an isolation and self-enclosure that can modulate in value toward either integrity or alienation; and a grounding unification that yet retains individual differences within it. Creeley has drawn forth some of these implications of *one* in the first section of "Numbers":

> *One*
>
> What
> singular upright flourishing
> condition . . .
> it enters here,
> it returns here.
>
> .
>
> Who was I that
> thought it was
> another one by
> itself divided or multiplied
> produces one.
>
> .
>
> This time, this
> place, this
> one.
>
> .
>
> You are not
> me, nor I you.
>
> .
>
> All ways.
>
> .
>
> As of a stick,
> stone, some-

thing so
fixed it has

a head, walks,
talks, leads

a life.[4]

The many, contradictory senses of *one* are not resolved in Creeley's writing into a dialectical unity, for he wants it "all ways." But in "This World," "what / matters" for Creeley (in a formulation reminiscent of Williams's "so much depends / upon") is to remain both "one" and "in this world," continually enacting the subject's questioning of the ground.

"TO *REALIZE* THE WORLD ANEW": FIVE ALTERNATIVE GROUNDING MODES

Reflecting on the following lines from Allen Ginsberg's "Song,"

yes, yes,
                    that's what
I wanted,
              I always wanted,
I always wanted,
                    to return
to the body
              where I was born.

Robert Creeley comments, "That body is the 'field' and is equally the experience of it. It is, then, to 'return' not to oneself as some egocentric center, but to experience oneself as *in* the world, thus, through this agency or fact we call, variously, 'poetry' " (QG, 63–4). Again, Creeley sees poetry as primarily enacting a return to the ground, to the body, to being-in-the-world. The question Creeley asks at the end of "This World," "What / matters as one / in this world?" is an existential question addressed not only to the issue of individual identity but also that of poetic identity, for it is "through this agency or fact we call, variously, 'poetry' " (notice the anxiety evident in the constant hedging around the claim to poetry) that one can, Creeley proposes, " 'return' . . . to experience oneself as *in* the world."

This meditation upon poetry as an act of grounding occurs in a lecture Creeley delivered in Berlin in 1967, "I'm given to write poems." In this lecture, he presented a European audience with his understanding of what is at stake in American poetry. I would like to use several points from this compact and perceptive lecture as a means to draw forth and reiterate the alternative grounding modes that this study has proposed as integral to American poetry. The following five modes have figured prominently in these pages: the idiosyncratic tradition, the poetic community, picture-writing, the inscription of place, and the uses of prose. With the help of Creeley's lecture, we can highlight these as distinct options employed, either separately or in concert, by a great number of American poets.

The idiosyncratic tradition of a Williams or an Eliot is, as the latter asserts, constructed "by great labour." Creeley also repeats this Promethean gesture of the culture-bringer in a curious confessional passage during his lecture:

> One of the few books I've ever had that was stolen – not by me, as it happened, but by a girl I persuaded to steal it for me – was William Carlos Williams' *The Wedge*. It proved *fire* of a very real order, and, for the record, was subsequently stolen from me in turn when I was teaching at Black Mountain in the fifties. In 1944, when it was first published and shortly after which I got hold of it, its content was a revelation to me. (QG, 64)

This passage encodes figuratively much of the struggle an American poet undergoes in "getting hold of" a tradition to authorize his or her poetry. In the first place, the standard romantic myth of the poet as a Promethean figure stealing fire is invoked. In contrast to the British Romantics, however, whose fire-stealing is a revolutionary act aimed at realigning cultural and political power within a traditional society, Creeley's antiheroic Promethean act (which the gallant knight sends his lady to perform!) involves the guilty stealing of an ancestor for his own benefit. As in primitive sorcery, the capture of the ancestor's power forms part of an inherently unstable economy: That power will inevitably be stolen by someone else in turn. Interestingly, the initial act of theft occurred when Creeley was eighteen or nineteen, while it was a decade later, when he had already taken his place as a central writer in the Black Mountain community, that the balance was redressed.

Claiming ancestry is an act of stealth for American poets: With no central firepit from which to draw his or her power, a poet is forced into self-authorization via symbolic theft; as Creeley says, the "revelation" he received occurred not simply from reading but from "getting hold of" Williams's text. Although such thievery procures only provisional authorization, the creation of an idiosyncratic tradition offers the society and other poets a number of boons. For example, although neither T. S. Eliot nor Ezra Pound accomplishes the sort of foundational epic achieved by Homer or Vergil, their incessant tradition-building enterprises bear many fruits: neglected texts are revived; new connections are made among a vast multitude of ideas, texts, and other works of art; the recurrent notion of America as a world-nation – the inheritor of all times and places – is brought into the twentieth century; a strong argument is made for universal esthetic standards, while the very heterogeneity of the examples that illustrate such standards protects them from a normative rigidity; the nineteenth-century model of the grounded poet as autochthonous, as a pristine product of the native soil, is replaced by the more hermeneutically satisfying model of poet as translator; and, finally, the great syncretic poetry of *The Waste Land* and *The Cantos* is written. Obeying Hermes, each American poet must not only sing but, when it comes to tradition, act the thief. With time, an Emersonian lineage, or thieves' gallery, has emerged, which, although not yet a tradition, begins to sketch out for our poets a number of successful modes of grounding.

Creeley's transformation from the position of an orphaned child (relying upon a sororal figure to steal the poetic sustenance for him) to that of a teacher at Black Mountain College (a member of a poetic community) was effected in large part through his often daily correspondence with Olson and a number of other poets. After a passage in his lecture that testifies to the power of books to create a home for him in an otherwise hostile world ("I used books as a very real *place* to be" [QG, 62]), Creeley then invokes the expanded sense of belonging he felt with another member of the Black Mountain group, Robert Duncan: "let me note kinship with another writer – Robert Duncan – who has played a very important role in my life, both as mentor, very often, and as one whom I feel to share with me this particular sense of world, and writing, and poetry, which I most deeply respect" (QG, 62). Because the traditional lineage of culture, with its central institution of the master–disciple relationship, has been abrogated in American culture, poets can often be found seeking counsel and support from their comrades. This produces a particular kind of creative confusion that Duncan exemplifies at length in his *H.D. Book*. When the generational boundaries are uncertain, the fathers (for Duncan, poets such as Pound and Williams) are open to constant revision, while the siblings (such as Olson, Creeley, and Levertov) are invoked as authorities:[5]

> Since [the conventional critic] has no other conceivable route to knowledge of [Robert Creeley's] work, taste must suffice. But I can have no recourse to taste. The work of Denise Levertov or Robert Creeley or Larry Eigner belongs not to my appreciations but to my immediate concerns in living. That I might "like" or "dislike" a poem of Zukofsky's or Charles Olson's means nothing where I turn to their work as evidence of the real. Movement and associa-

tion here are not arbitrary, but arise as an inner need. I can no more rest with my impressions of *Maximus* than I can indulge my impressions at any vital point: I must study thru, deepen my experience, search out the challenge and salvation of the work. (*FC,* 104)

The poet's drive for authorization leads him or her to place value in ways that have bewildered conventional critics, for the poet's reading is informed by the "inner need" for a grounding association with the community rather than by normative esthetic standards. The community expands upon the sense of "home" that Creeley noted he found in books; the kinds of reassurance and mutual criticism offered by the members of such a fraternity greatly extend the initial authorization for writing found in one's reading. Not only do several other human beings take one and one's intentions seriously, but the members of a community, through letters, journals, mutual criticism, and social occasions, also help define in much greater detail for a poet "a very real *place* to be." The poetic community both binds and frees, exacting allegiance and granting permission. Speaking of the Black Mountain group, Duncan said: "I did understand that there was an immense impetus that would be important to me in the sense of having contemporaries – I wouldn't have to cover everything in my own writing. I could be increasingly on my own, providing there was a Creeley also writing and people would be reading us together."[6]

The American anxiety that "I would have to cover everything in my own writing," that fear of groundlessness and isolation, has been allayed to some extent for poets by the mutual recognition that they are working alongside one another, "covering" different portions of the ground, circling it like pioneers in a wagon train at night.[7] Within the Emersonian lineage, groups such as the transcendentalists, the modernists, the objectivists, the projectivists, the Beats, and the Language poets have all created communities of one sort or another. The social power and permission offered the poet can be quite effective in making the writing of American poetry seem possible. Edgar Allan Poe provides an interesting example of an ambitious poet who suffered under the apprehension of having to cover everything in his own writing: Lacking the permission to innovate conferred upon him by a sympathetic community, he became fixated on the authoritative stature of English formal excellence; thus, he overcultivated the formal qualities of his own verse and insisted upon formal issues in his criticism with a stridency that compensated for that lack. By contrast, much of the formal innovation in American poetry has been sustained through the mutual encouragement of a group of poets. The most fully documented American poetic community is probably that of the Black Mountain poets between 1950 and 1970 (when Olson died); reading the correspondence of these poets makes it clear that the anxiety, the isolation, and the uncertainty of whether poetry was even possible had not disappeared from the American scene by the mid-twentieth century. However, the achievement of these poets during the time the community flourished was quite remarkable, and it is interest-ing to observe how, in the years following the dissolution of the group, poets like Duncan, Creeley, Levertov, and Dorn set off in new directions, not all of which were immediately fruitful.

The two grounding methods of the poetic community and the idio-syncratic tradition can be combined together in a way that may anticipate the evolution of a more stable Emersonian tradition in American poetry. In welcoming a younger writer, Richard Grossinger, into the projectivist fold, Robert Duncan introduced Grossinger's first book by placing him in a tradition of poetic communities:

> In writing on *Maximus* in 1954 I worked out from a quote from Emerson's *Hamatraya,* with the sense that when it was realized how deeply I was Emersonian and in turn when our vision of our genius was enlarged to see how Emerson and Melville, Hawthorne (cen-tral to an understanding of Spicer and Robin Blaser), Emily Dickin-son (Creeley, Eigner), and Whitman – how these five form a con-stellation – then the full promise of our rebirth in Poetry would be released.[8]

Positing Grossinger's work as a fulfillment of transcendentalist and pro-jectivist modes of grounding, Duncan imagines an American "genius" that is reincarnated in successive poetic "constellations," whose job is to recognize more and more fully the implications of America's peculiar relationship to tradition.

Acknowledging the singular condition that faces American poets, Creeley speaks of the content or doctrine of the poetic community, which involves a new relationship of word to thing: "It may well be that in the absence of such allusive society as European literature, in its own condition, has necessarily developed, that the American in contrast must so realize each specific thing of his own – 'as though it had never / happened before' " (*QG,* 69). Creeley places added stress upon this ac-tivity of "realization" when he says of Americans that "they feel that they, perhaps more than any other group upon the earth at this moment, have had both to imagine and thereby to *make* that reality which they are then given to live in. It is as though they had to *realize* the world anew. They are, as Charles Olson says, 'the last first people' " (*QG,* 65). How does one, in the absence of a grounding tradition, "realize the world anew"? The word *realize* has both creative and receptive connotations, as though there were a cooperation in the poet between an openness to the

world and an interpretive imposition upon it. To realize something
means both seeing what is there and making that recognition apparent.
We must "realize the world anew" because we do not trust the realizations handed down by tradition.

Ultimately, this is an issue of language, for language contains our
realizations of the world. American poetic cults from the Puritans to the
present have given allegiance to the broad doctrine we have called
"picture-writing," the doctrine stating that words for things also signify
inward reality. In European culture, the Greco-Christian Logos *is* tradition and authority, and it issues in scripture and other canonical texts.
The American relationship to the word is identifiably different; since
words do not speak to us with the absolute authority of divinity or
tradition, with meanings grounded and sanctioned in an ultimate reality,
American writers have sought to ground them in the clearing where
nature and experience meet. Whitman states this doctrine succinctly in
"Song of Myself": "To me the converging objects of the universe perpetually flow, / All are written to me, and I must get what the writing
means" (*LG,* 47). Olson also proposes this American relationship to the
word, in which meaning is conjectural rather than absolutely sanctioned,
when he begins "Human Universe" by advocating a hieroglyphic use of
language as an alternative to the Logos. In approaching the phenomeno-
logical "human universe" that Olson wishes to substitute for the universe
as given us by tradition (which he calls "the universe of discourse"), we
must remain aware

> that definition is as much a part of the act as is sensation itself, in
> this sense, that life *is* preoccupation with itself, that conjecture
> about it is as much of it as its coming at us, its going on. In other
> words, we are ourselves both the instrument of discovery and the
> instrument of definition.
>
> Which is, of course, why language is a prime of the matter and
> why, if we are to see some of the laws afresh, it is necessary to
> examine, first, the present condition of the language – and I mean
> language exactly in its double sense of discrimination (logos) and of
> shout (tongue).
>
> We have long lived in a generalizing time, at least since 450 B.C.
> And it has had its effects on the best of men, on the best of things.
> Logos, or discourse, for example, has, in that time, so worked its
> abstractions into our concept and use of language that language's
> other function, speech, seems so in need of restoration that several
> of us got back to hieroglyphs or to ideograms to right the balance.
> (The distinction here is between language as the act of the instant
> and language as the act of thought about the instant.) (*SW,* 53–4)

In traditional cultures, symbols control words, so that by following the graded levels of interpretation (such as the four Dante recommends) one can use the symbol to reach the Logos. In America, words are not so tightly governed by symbols but are seen to have a numinous quality of their own, which invites acts of conjecture that illuminate simultaneously the inner and outer realms of experience and nature. Using terms such as *typology, hieroglyph,* and *ideogram,* writers and critics have demonstrated the importance of picture-writing in virtually every period of American literature. H.D., for instance, demonstrates the visionary synthesis underlying Imagism in her lifelong exploration of the image as hieroglyph, palimpsest, and "writing on the wall." American poets have looked for a substitute scripture in words as hieratic objects, believing that words are the meeting ground of the inner and outer worlds. Emerson is the fountainhead of this mystique of the word, arguing in *Nature* that the hieroglyphic quality of words gives more direct access to the truth than does endlessly mediated tradition.

Attempts to read the truth in nature, though, are always fraught with the danger of one's merely finding there by projection whatever one announced oneself to be seeking: A truth of this sort must be rather reductive and trivial. Recognizing this potential pitfall, American poets progressively have come to employ an objectivist "realization" of the world through offering the words in their poetry as things, facts, or objects. Gradually, the symbolic content of picture-writing has given way to a notion of the hieroglyph as self-predicating, as "that which exists through itself." Starting with Pound, Williams, Stein, Moore, and Loy, and continuing in the objectivists, the projectivists, and now the Language poets, the American poet's "realization" of the world has come to be dominated more and more by an investigation of language, in which the word is presented as a form of picture-writing, substituting its recognitive and creative capacities for the grounding voice of tradition. Along with the idiosyncratic tradition, picture-writing is the mode of grounding that most directly intersects with the other main enterprise of American poetry, which is modernism. Although picture-writing can create new grounding contexts by bringing inner and outer worlds into alignment, it can also embrace more fully than other modes the rupture of the modern and thus work to isolate and apotheosize individual words and phrases.

Some of the most extended treatments of the grounding ability of picture-writing occur in texts whose central grounding strategy is the exploration of a place. Preeminently, three books illustrate how place can function as ground for American poetry: *Walden, Paterson,* and *The Maximus Poems.* While tradition always has a metaphysical focus, it usually has a central geographical location as well: Benares, Jerusalem, Mecca,

Athens, Rome, Macchu Picchu, Benin, Paris, London, and so on. Confronted with the lack of such a metaphysical center, Americans have displayed the anxiety of a provincial.[9] Poets like Dickinson and Williams, for instance, had so little faith in America as a place with the cultural riches capable of sustaining major poetry that the former refrained altogether from publishing her astonishing oeuvre, while the anxiety of the latter, apparent throughout his career in attempts to define and defend a nativist esthetic, broke forth at a most precarious place (the bridge between El Paso and Juarez) in his late poem, "The Desert Music": "I *am* a poet! I / am. I am. I am a poet, I reaffirmed, ashamed."[10] Commenting on this quote, Creeley says: "In America, we are certainly not poets simply, nor much of the time. . . . And I'm even awkward about using that designation, that is, to call myself so, a poet – because I do not feel I have that decision in it. Yet the complexity of the dilemma seems to me a very real one" (*QG,* 69). Questions like "Is America a place for poetry?" or "Is there a place in America for poetry?" do not go away.

Looking at the places chosen for extended consideration by Thoreau, Williams, and Olson – Walden Pond, Paterson, and Gloucester – we see that the poets have situated themselves in locales that make no pretense to cultural centrality. Instead, they explore these decidedly marginal locations in the hope that an anticosmopolitan geographical grounding may provide a hieroglyphic (as opposed to logocentric) verticality of layers, an integral ladder from the minute particular to the largest issues. This objectivist ladder occurs not only in the three poets mentioned but also in Whitman, Pound, Louis Zukofsky, George Oppen, Denise Levertov, Edward Dorn, Gary Snyder, Susan Howe, and others. In the course of writing whole books about placement, Thoreau, Williams, and Olson move through three levels of engagement with the place: a pacing of the actual ground; a gauging of the human activities that occur upon it; and a posing of principles consonant with the lessons learned by extended attention to the place. In seeking to reground metaphors in reality, as Emerson urged, these poets explore their places through complex and extensive episodes of picture-writing.

In addition, the American poetry of place, because it has had no traditional cosmopolis for reference, has attempted to counter a groundless relativism through positing a self-existent locus, an Archimedean point, and then measuring the rest of the world in relation to it. The early fishermen of Gloucester, for instance, in their individuality, their political unity, and their care for nature, become a measure for the subsequent decline of American culture and, ultimately, are made to constellate around themselves the major achievements of the human species. These activities of placement, relation, and measurement are central to Emersonian poetics. And not only is geographical location at issue but metrical placement as well. The "field" spoken of by poets like Pound, Williams, Olson, Duncan, and Creeley is an alternate ground to the stanzaic measures provided by traditional poetics. Discussions of poetics by all of these poets are so freighted with metaphysics because the act of measurement involves placement upon a ground. Creeley's contention that the ability to write poetry is a matter of placement receives confirmation in Duncan's poem, "OFTEN I AM PERMITTED TO RETURN TO A MEADOW," whose opening Creeley quotes:

> as if it were a scene made-up by the mind,
> that is not mine, but is a made place,
>
> that is mine, it is so near to the heart,
> an eternal pasture folded in all thought
> so that there is a hall therein
>
> that is a made place, created by light
> wherefrom the shadows that are forms fall.

This sense of a poem – that *place*, that *meadow* – has echoes of so many things that are intimate to my own sense of the reality experienced in writing. One would find that field or "meadow" in Whitman also, and it would be equally the sense of place I feel Allen Ginsberg many times to be entering, to be speaking of or longing for. Charles Olson too proposes its occasion in his sense of "open" verse or that *open field*, as he insists upon it, in composition. I have found it deeply in H.D.'s writing: "I go where I love and am loved. . . ." And in Pound's "What thou lovest well remains, / the rest is dross." . . .

All of these are, to my own mind, not only tokens but evidences of a place, a very distinct and definite *place*, that poetry not only creates but itself issues from – and one in writing is, as Duncan says, "permitted to return," to go there, to be in that reality. (QG, 62–3)

For Creeley, placement involves esthetic, emotional, and metaphysical concerns. One could say that the extraterritorial situation of so many European and other writers in the world today also invests the issue of placement with a similar weight. The difference, however, is that for American writers this act of placement is an initial condition rather than a symptom of recent dislocation. Possibly the only analogue to the American situation of original displacement would be the Jewish tradition of homelessness. For the Jews, though, there has always remained a sacred geography, divinely sanctioned, that has accompanied them throughout their wanderings.

The need not only to distinguish American poets from others but also to announce their very presence is in itself a central preoccupation of our poets. Self-annunciatory prose such as Creeley's in "I'm given to write poems" is by no means exceptional. Throughout this book I have dwelt primarily upon such prose because it provides one of the most important forms of alternative grounding. Within this prose the poets attempt to construct their own background, against which their poetry will function with meaning. Writing in a prosaic age, so many of our poets feel that their poetry must find sanction in prose; and as readers we feel the same thing. If central essays like Emerson's "The Poet," Whitman's 1855 "Preface" and "A Backward Glance," Eliot's "Tradition and the Individual Talent," Pound's "A Retrospect," "How to Read," and his Fenollosa edition, and Olson's "Projective Verse" and "Human Universe" were stripped away from American poetry, the poetry would appear literally groundless; it is arguable whether without these essays the poetry would make any sense to us. So much of the *work* of American poetry has, necessarily, taken place in prose of all kinds – polemical, explanatory, autobiographical, historical, fictional, and poetic (poet's prose). Prose is a major part of the ongoing effort of grounding American poetry.

Finally, though, poetry is possible. Although in an odd and unacknowledged way, tradition functions in America too. Creeley begins his essay with a celebration of the uncanny ability to write poetry:

> I'm *given* to write poems. I cannot anticipate their occasion. I have used all the intelligence that I can muster to follow the possibilities that the poem "underhand," as Olson would say, is declaring, but I cannot anticipate the necessary conclusions of the activity, nor can I judge in any sense, in moments of writing, the significance of that writing more than to recognize that it is being *permitted* to continue. I'm trying to say that, in writing, at least as I have experienced it, one is *in* the activity, and that fact itself is what I feel so deeply the significance of anything we call poetry. (QG, 61)

In America one is not offered the traditional givens of cultural authority and sanction, neither ways or means of writing nor approved subjects for treatment, but somehow tradition, in the most mysterious sense, holds open the possibility of writing. This is the only given in the American tradition. In celebrating this nakedly existential possibility, Creeley embraces what writers in most societies would find an inconceivable lack, an authoritative absence of huge proportions. There is, though, a kind of authority that arises from reveling in such a lack, for it moves one into direct relationship with the powerful withholding quality of tradition. To meet this quality, Whitman explores in "Out of the Cradle" what he calls "the sweet hell within, / The unknown want, the destiny of me" (ll.

156–7), recognizing that his destiny as an American poet is fundamentally tied to the "sweet hell" that tradition withholds. By casting their lot with the deathly lack that resides at the heart of tradition, American poets are given an unanticipated access to an unforeseen truth. As Creeley puts it: "what emerges in the writing I value most is a content which cannot be anticipated, which 'tells you what you don't know,' which you subvert, twist, or misrepresent only on peril of death" (QG, 72). In America, tradition is not closed but open, not given but recognized, not agreed upon as a norm but disclosed as a secret. By situating themselves directly within the rupture of the modern, American poets encounter the condition of groundlessness head-on and with dead seriousness. The great gift of this writing is that it "tells you what you don't know."

NOTES

INTRODUCTION

1. To place the American poets' relationship with Gerhardt and his magazine in the context of their attempts to define a poetic and political platform and to publish their work, see *Charles Olson and Robert Creeley: The Complete Correspondence,* ed. George F. Butterick, 9 vols. (Santa Barbara, Calif.: Black Sparrow Press, 1980–), esp. 4: 26–34 and 125–8.

2. Rainer M. Gerhardt, "Letter for Creeley and Olson," trans. Werner Heider and Joanna Jalowetz, *Origin* 1.4 (1952): 190–1.

3. *Poet's Prose: The Crisis in American Verse,* 2d ed. (Cambridge: Cambridge Univ. Press, 1990).

4. Stanley Cavell, "Thinking of Emerson," *Senses,* 137.

1. WILLIAMS, ELIOT, AND AMERICAN TRADITION

1. William Carlos Williams, *Selected Essays* (1954; rpt. New York: New Directions, 1969), 143. In the opening chapter of *The Tenth Muse: The Psyche of the American Poet* (Cambridge, Mass.: Harvard Univ. Press, 1975), Albert Gelpi gives a graphic account of the difficulties American poets have had in starting out, particularly with English critics sitting in judgment upon them: "Consequently, seldom – perhaps never before – have a nation's poets been as consistently concerned with and self-conscious about their purpose and their role as American poets have been – indeed have had to be – from the start. . . . Thrown back on himself more than his counterpart in England or the continent, the American is forced to name his identity on his own ground and root his speech in that self-defined ground" (10). Roy Harvey Pearce also notes "the American poet's compulsion (or obligation) again and again to justify his existence as poet" (*The Continuity of American Poetry* [Princeton, N.J.: Princeton Univ. Press, 1960], 4).

2. A striking example of the intimacy felt by people within a tradition for its towering monuments would be the recent weekly television airing of the *Mahabharata* in India, which seemingly attracted the entire country to view each of the countless episodes. It was not uncommon for whole neigh-

borhoods or villages to converge upon TV sets, as though huddling around a fire to listen to a storyteller.

3. Charles Olson, *Letters for Origin: 1950–1956,* ed. Albert Glover (New York: Cape Goliard Press, 1970), 8; rpt. Charles Olson and Cid Corman, *Complete Correspondence: 1950–1964,* ed. George Evans (Orono, Me.: National Poetry Foundation, 1987), 1: 42–3.

4. Stanley Cavell, "Reply to Gayatri Spivak," in W. J. T. Mitchell, ed., *The Politics of Interpretation* (Chicago: Univ. of Chicago Press, 1983), 201–2; rpt. Stanley Cavell, *Themes Out of School: Effects and Causes* (Chicago: Univ. of Chicago Press, 1984), 59.

5. Eliot's ungrounded notion of tradition as a collage gave birth to modernist education in the form of the Great Books or Humanities course, in which tradition is presented as a collage of dehistoricized, equivalent, English-language texts. Alasdair MacIntyre describes such a course as "a museum of texts, each rendered contextless and therefore other than its original by being placed on a cultural pedestal. . . ." Our hope regarding such texts is that "the reading of them would reintegrate modern students into what is thought of as *our* tradition, that unfortunate fictitious amalgam sometimes known as 'the Judeo-Christian tradition' and sometimes as 'Western values.' The writings of self-proclaimed contemporary conservatives, such as William J. Bennett, turn out in fact to be one more stage in modernity's cultural deformation of our relationship to the past." Alasdair MacIntyre, *Whose Justice? Which Rationality?* (Notre Dame, Ind.: Univ. of Notre Dame Press, 1988), 385–6.

6. *Saturday Review of Literature* 2.21 (December 1925); rpt. Charles Doyle, ed., *William Carlos Williams: The Critical Heritage* (London: Routledge & Kegan Paul, 1980), 84–6.

7. Steven Ross Loevy, "Introduction to William Carlos Williams's *Rome,*" *Iowa Review* 9.3 (1978): 5.

8. J. Hillis Miller, *Poets of Reality: Six Twentieth-Century Writers* (Cambridge, Mass.: Harvard Univ. Press, 1966): 328–9.

9. Bryce Conrad, *Refiguring America: A Study of William Carlos Williams'* In the American Grain (Urbana: Univ. of Illinois Press, 1990), 19–20.

10. Conrad discusses Williams's debt to Emerson for the impulse to "center all knowledge of history in the immediate fact of one's present existence" (21). Olson will develop this methodology further as a central feature of his practice of containment.

11. Martin Heidegger, "The Question Concerning Technology," in *Basic Writings,* ed. David Krell (New York: Harper & Row, 1977), 283–317.

12. Gerald L. Bruns, "What Is Tradition?" *New Literary History* 22 (1991): 8.

13. David Antin, "Some Questions about Modernism," *Occident* 8 (n.s.) (Spring 1974): 7–38; see esp. 18–26.

14. For a detailed scholarly reading of the poem, see George Butterick, "Charles Olson's 'The Kingfishers' and the Poetics of Change," *American Poetry* 6.2 (1988): 28–69. There is further material of interest in Clark, 146–8.

15. This sense of the earth as withholding seems similar to Heidegger's pitting

of earth against world in "The Origin of the Work of Art." See Gerald Bruns's discussion of this essay in chapter 1 of his *Heidegger's Estrangements: Language, Truth, and Poetry in the Later Writings* (New Haven: Yale Univ. Press, 1989).

16. In a draft of the poem, Olson asks, "where, among the stones, lie the tradition?" before asserting "I hunt among stones" (Butterick, "Olson's 'The Kingfishers,' " 53).

17. "Scholia and Conjectures for 'The Kingfishers,' " in Guy Davenport, *The Geography of the Imagination* (San Francisco: North Point Press, 1981), 89. Sherman Paul, *Olson's Push: Origin, Black Mountain, and Recent American Poetry* (Baton Rouge: Louisiana State Univ. Press, 1978), 17. Laszlo Géfin, *Ideogram: History of a Poetic Method* (Austin: Univ. of Texas Press, 1982), ix.

18. "The Kingfishers" and "The Praises" were originally linked sections of a long poem called *Proteus* or *The Proteid*, which, as its title suggests, explores the relationship of "the will to change" (*CP*, 86) to the hiddenness of tradition. See Butterick, "Olson's 'The Kingfishers,' " 52–9, and Clark, 146.

19. "The Rites of Participation" (*H.D. Book*, pt. 1, chap. 6), *Caterpillar* 1 (1967): 26.

2. FINDING OUT FOR ONESELF

1. Walter Benn Michaels, "*Walden*'s False Bottoms," *Glyph* 1.1 (1977): 135. Hereafter cited as *WFB*.

2. The objectivists, a group of poets in the late 1920s and early 1930s consisting primarily of William Carlos Williams, Louis Zukofsky, Charles Reznikoff, George Oppen, Lorine Niedecker, Carl Rakosi, and English poet Basil Bunting, sought to further imagist principles by insisting upon the complementary concreteness of things, words, and the poem itself. For an incisive discussion of Thoreau's anticipation of imagism and objectivism, see H. Daniel Peck, *Thoreau's Morning Work: Memory and Perception in* A Week on the Concord and Merrimack Rivers, *the Journal, and* Walden (New Haven: Yale Univ. Press, 1990), 69–75. The paradoxical conjunction of objectivism and transcendentalism can also be seen as an American version of the "natural supernaturalism" favored by nineteenth-century Romanticism.

3. Robert von Hallberg studies the relationship between Olson's scholarship, his politics, and his poetry in *Charles Olson: The Scholar's Art* (Cambridge, Mass.: Harvard Univ. Press, 1978). Tom Clark traces the origin of Olson's " 'saturation method' of documentary accumulation" to Frederick Merk's course at Harvard (1937–8) on Westward Movement (Clark, 47).

4. Olson attributes the passages in quotation marks to J. A. K. Thomson, *The Art of the Logos* (London: Allen & Unwin, 1935). Actually, as George Butterick points out in his *Guide to the Maximus Poems* (Berkeley: Univ. of California Press, 1978), 147, this whole passage is quoted directly from Thomson, 237. Olson consistently transcribes 'ιστορίη as 'istorin, sometimes inverting the aspiration mark.

5. Joan Burbick, *Thoreau's Alternative History: Changing Perspectives on Nature, Culture, and Language* (Philadelphia: Univ. of Pennsylvania Press, 1987), 16.

6. Sherman Paul, "Review of John Hildebidle, *Thoreau: A Naturalist's Liberty*," *Journal of English and Germanic Philology* 83 (1984): 461-2. H. Daniel Peck also compares Thoreau and Olson for their similar approaches to history (*Thoreau's Morning Work*, 19, 153).

7. As far back as 1947, Olson had given a lecture in Seattle, "Poetry and Criticism," in which he contended that, since "experience, like matter, is discontinuous," what we needed was, in Tom Clark's paraphrase, "a poetics based not on abstract ideas but on the solid building blocks of fact and document. The process of change would involve less an innovation of technique than a return to archaic means, with document taking over the onetime role of magic in human mystery, fact that of religious ritual" (Clark, 124).

8. Or could one even become a "representative woman"? Sadly (for it places a severe limitation upon their conceptions of human possibility), there seems little evidence to suggest that either Thoreau or Olson thought such a thing possible. But if we ask ourselves whether American women poets in the objectivist/transcendentalist lineage enact a relationship to the fact that displays a luminosity similar to that called for by the two male writers, the answer would be yes: consider, for example, the work of Emily Dickinson, Marianne Moore, H.D., Lorine Niedecker, Denise Levertov, and Hilda Morley. The question of whether, and upon what terms, these women might become "representative" is too large to consider here. We can note, however, that the most intriguing revelation in Tom Clark's biography of Olson regards the poet's cocreative relationship with writer–book designer Frances Boldereff, who made substantial contributions to Olson's imagery, ideas, and themes, and served as muse and interlocutor for much of his writing (see esp. 145–74).

9. Keats's famous letters discussing the Egotistical Sublime and Negative Capability formed one of the primary touchstones for Olson's thinking. They are a central matter for meditation throughout *The Special View of History*, beginning with the epigraph on Negative Capability. William Spanos asserts the connection of Heidegger's *Gelassenheit* (letting be) to Keats's Negative Capability in a chapter of his *Repetitions: The Postmodern Occasion in Literature and Culture* (Baton Rouge: Louisiana State Univ. Press, 1987), entitled "Charles Olson and Negative Capability: A De-structive Interpretation" (107–47). See also Paul Bové, *Destructive Poetics: Heidegger and Modern American Poetry* (New York: Columbia Univ. Press, 1980), 243–44, 255–57. In this connection, I would also like to mention Joseph Riddel's avowedly poststructuralist reading of Olson, "Decentering the Image: The 'Project' of 'American' Poetics?" in Josué Harari, ed., *Textual Strategies: Perspectives in Post-Structuralist Criticism* (Ithaca, N.Y.: Cornell Univ. Press, 1979), 322–58.

10. In a rich meditation on the factors of "Birds, Landscape, Place, and Cosmicity" in Olson, Sherman Paul gives a suggestive discussion of the nest image in *The Maximus Poems*. Citing Bachelard on the childhood associa-

tions of a nest with both self-making and world-making, Paul speaks of the nest as "the model of poem, polis, and cosmos." He then comments upon the similar nest-making of Thoreau at Walden Pond and speculates that Olson was silent about Thoreau because Olson had already overcome the Romantic dualism that Thoreau constantly struggled against. Paul also notes that although Thoreau was "the writer whose concern with place equals his and whose work in so many ways is comparable with his own," Olson differed from him in choosing the polis rather than nature as the location for his nest. Sherman Paul, *Hewing to Experience: Essays and Reviews on Recent American Poetry and Poetics, Nature and Culture* (Iowa City: Univ. of Iowa Press, 1989), 214–15, 222.

11. The sexual nature of the relationship between the "tender mast" that Maximus "struts" and the nest of containment has a biographical origin. The poem "I, Maximus" began in a letter to Olson's lover, Frances Boldereff, written to celebrate a recent night spent together. Curiously, the image of the nest arose from Olson's subconscious as a typing error: he substituted *s* for *x* when retyping in verse, for her, a meditation on the risks of trusting to spontaneity in projective verse:

> the thing may lie
> around the bend of the nest
> second . . .

See Clark, 165–8.

12. Butterick attributes the origin of this remark to Dahlberg in his *Guide*, 16.

13. "Inside Out," in Robert Creeley, *Was That a Real Poem and Other Essays,* ed. Donald Allen (Bolinas, Calif.: Four Seasons Foundation, 1979), 57 (ellipsis Creeley's). For a fuller discussion of Creeley's notion of autobiography, see my *Poet's Prose,* 77–98.

14. D. H. Lawrence was a major influence on Olson's views of sex. See Olson's review of Lawrence's *The Man Who Died,* "The Escaped Cock" (*HU* 123–5). Ekbert Faas discusses Olson's relation to Lawrence in *Towards a New American Poetics: Essay and Interviews* (Santa Barbara, Calif.: Black Sparrow Press, 1978), 39–51. And Tom Clark notes that Olson owned and displayed above his writing desk a small watercolor by Lawrence, depicting "a naked man urinating into a bank of daffodils" (160–1).

15. Olson's perceptions of love and flesh place him, again, in line with D. H. Lawrence and, before Lawrence, with Walt Whitman. See Lawrence's adulation and revision of Whitman in *Studies in Classic American Literature* (1923; rpt. New York: Viking Press, 1964), 163–77.

16. This meditation upon the spectator is deeply informed, as the allusion to the Hindu sky-god Indra indicates, by Thoreau's immersion in Eastern scriptures, especially the *Bhagavad-Gita*. In a passage at the beginning of the *Gita,* which also inspired Emerson's poem "Brahma," Lord Krishna informs Arjuna that there is a deep self, which is merely a spectator to "the play, it may be the tragedy, of life":

> He who thinks this self a killer
> and he who thinks it killed,

> both fail to understand;
> it does not kill, nor is it killed.
>
> It is not born,
> it does not die;
> having been,
> it will never not be;
> unborn, enduring,
> constant, and primordial,
> it is not killed
> when the body is killed.
>
> . . . .
>
> As a man discards
> worn-out clothes
> to put on new
> and different ones,
> so the embodied self
> discards
> its worn-out bodies
> to take on other new ones.

The Bhagavad-Gita: Krishna's Counsel in Time of War, trans. Barbara Stoler Miller (New York: Bantam, 1986), 32, (II.19–22). For a succinct assessment of the Gita's influence on Thoreau, see Miller's "Afterword: Why Did Henry David Thoreau Take the Bhagavad-Gita to Walden Pond?"

17. Paul, Olson's Push, 118.
18. William V. Spanos, "Talking with Robert Creeley," boundary 2 6/7 (1978): 39–40. The odd spacing was supplied by Spanos, in imitation of David Antin's breath-unit notation. Following Creeley's anecdote, Spanos goes on to note that Olson's experience of containment, as he describes it in The Mayan Letters and "Human Universe," also occurs among the Mayans. Creeley considered this meeting with what he calls an "inexplicably contained person" so significant that he recounted the story again in his Autobiography (New York: Hanuman Books, 1990), 81–2.

3.   RESISTANCE AND POETIC COMMUNITY

1. Whitman uses a similar architectural image to speak of the certainty that arises from locating oneself in the body; out of this certainty arises an apprehension of the mysterious doubleness of the witness: "Sure as the most certain sure, plumb in the uprights, well entretied, braced in the beams, / Stout as a horse, affectionate, haughty, electrical, / I and this mystery here we stand" (LG, 31).
2. Don Byrd, Charles Olson's Maximus (Urbana: Univ. of Illinois, 1980), xiii. Olson received a firsthand demonstration of what Clark calls "the invasive authority of state power" in 1952, when two FBI men came to question him about his political activities in the mid-forties. Olson was profoundly shaken by the incident: "henceforth state power would be defined in his

imagination in absolute opposition to the authority of self in which he placed all faith" (Clark, 217–19). This was a significant political shift for a New Deal Democrat.

3.   Von Hallberg also relates Olson's belief in the power of a small community to change the world to the use of Mao in "The Kingfishers." *Charles Olson: The Scholar's Art,* 17–18.

4.   See Butterick's note on Olson's source for this phrase in *Olson: The Journal of the Charles Olson Archive* 3 (1975): 63.

5.   Byrd, *Charles Olson's Maximus,* x.

6.   Charles Boer records a revealing conversation between Olson and a student in the English department at the University of Connecticut, Blanche Adams, who was waiting on tables: "She sat at the table with you as you ate, as the other waitresses often did. You asked her how she felt about being a waitress. When she replied that she liked it, you advised her not to go on to graduate school in English. 'Keep waiting,' you said" (Boer, 102–3). This may not have been the first time in her life that this young woman was told to "Keep waiting." Olson was not in the habit of acknowledging the intellectual powers of women. For instance, the woman he relied upon for crucial intellectual and emotional nurturance, Frances Boldereff, was never given credit publicly by Olson for any of her contributions to his work (see Clark, 145–74). From another perspective, though, Olson's advice to the student makes it clear that he saw no indignity in the work of waitressing, which, like fishing and writing, he felt could reward all the care and attention one can bring to it.

Don Byrd, in an ambitious new book, *The Poetics of the Common Knowledge* (Albany: State Univ. of New York Press, forthcoming), develops an Olsonian epistemology that can, he claims, successfully negotiate between the excesses of cybernetics and poststructuralism. Rather than seeing knowledge primarily as manipulable information or, alternatively, as irremediably undermined by skepticism, Byrd follows Olson and the objectivist line of American poets in asserting that knowledge must be both discoverable and active in daily life.

7.   Jacob Needleman, *The Heart of Philosophy* (1982; rpt. New York: Bantam, 1984), 45.

8.   *The Secret of the Golden Flower,* trans. from Richard Wilhelm's German by Cary F. Baynes (New York: Harcourt, Brace & World, 1962), 21.

9.   In his *Guide,* Butterick identifies the date as June 17, 1958 (240). For another description of the dream, see Clark, 280–1.

10.   Compare Olson's image of the Black Chrysanthemum to Heidegger's etymological understanding of *physis* (nature or being):

> [*Physis*] denotes self-blossoming emergence (e.g., the blossoming of a rose), opening up, unfolding, that which manifests itself in such unfolding and perseveres and endures in it. . . .
> *Physis* as emergence can be observed everywhere, e.g., in celestial phenomena (the rising of the sun), in the rolling of the sea, in the growth of plants, in the coming forth of man and animal from the womb. . . .
> The opening up and inward-jutting-beyond-itself <in-sich-aus-sich-

hinausstehen> must not be taken as a process among other processes that we observe in the realm of the essent. *Physis* is being itself, by virtue of which essents become and remain observable.

An Introduction to Metaphysics, trans. Ralph Manheim (New Haven: Yale Univ. Press, 1959), 14.

11. Underscoring the importance of Olson's visionary strain in the last decade of his life, Tom Clark claims that he became a religious poet:

> Adopting a religious attitude he ascribed to "the ANCIENTS" (that "world outside and before Christianity" plus such isolated "EXCEPTIONS inside it circum 1200 A.D." as the alchemists and Arab and Vedic philosophers), following the semimystical autonomic discipline of self-measure, and intent to "write a poem simply to create a mode of priesthood in a church forever," Olson became during these years an intuitive dogmatist of private vision, a shamanic votary as committed to his own spiritual exercises as the Greek poet-priests to the mysteries of the earth goddess they guarded at Eleusis. ("All night long / I was a Eumolpidae / as I slept / putting things together / which had not previously fit.") (Clark, 282).

12. Edited, with notes and a facsimile, by George Butterick in *Olson* 3 (1975): 64–92. Reprinted in Charles Stein, *The Secret of the Black Chrysanthemum: The Poetic Cosmology of Charles Olson and His Use of the Writings of C. G. Jung* (Barrytown, N.Y.: Station Hill Press, 1987), 165–96. Stein uses "The Secret of the Black Chrysanthemum" as the central instigation for a study of Olson's debt to and reconfiguration of Jung; see especially pp. 156–9 for a discussion of the Black Chrysanthemum in relation to "Experience and Measurement."

13. Peter Berger, *Invitation to Sociology* (New York: Anchor, 1963), 132.

14. For a sensitive treatment of Thoreau's attempt to counter the condition of exile by writing himself into a sense of "at-homeness," see Frederick Garber, *Thoreau's Fable of Inscribing* (Princeton, N.J.: Princeton Univ. Press, 1991).

15. For a study of a poetic community parallel to that of Black Mountain, see Michael Davidson, *The San Francisco Renaissance: Poetics and Community at Mid-century* (Cambridge: Cambridge Univ. Press, 1989). An example of the lack of insularity of such poetic communities, Robert Duncan participated in both the Black Mountain and the San Francisco communities.

16. Illustrating the constant rivalry the projectivists encouraged between themselves and other schools of poetry, Tom Clark offers an anecdote from Richard Wilbur:

> Olson and Wilbur, nominated in a recent article as leaders of contending schools of verse, were formally introduced at a cocktail party later in the festival. Olson, outwardly "hearty" but immediately on his guard, lost no time in interjecting a note of challenge. Wilbur was struck by the confrontational energy with which his fellow poet seemed to address the occasion. "He greeted me as a coach or quarterback might greet the coach

or quarterback of a rival team. There was no implication that my school of poetry was a wrong or misguided school; he was more generous about that than I have ever known some other Black Mountain poets to be; but it was clear that he *did* think in terms of rival schools and aesthetics." (Clark, 290)

17. Other writers, both in and out of the projectivist group, also worked in close association with these three poets. Within the group, the two other members whose participation was most crucial to its development were Denise Levertov and Ed Dorn. Wishing not to minimize the extent of their contributions and the value of their poetry, I have reluctantly excluded them from significant treatment in this study because of considerations of space and methodology.

18. See Paul, *Hewing to Experience*, 257–311, for a careful reviewing of the first eight volumes of *Charles Olson and Robert Creeley: The Complete Correspondence*. Don Byrd, in "The Question of Wisdom as Such," in Robert Bertholf and Ian Reid, eds., *Robert Duncan: Scales of the Marvelous* (New York: New Directions, 1979), 38–55, describes the fruitful relations between Duncan and Olson as originating in an opposition of "the fictionalist versus the literalist" (38–9).

19. Jed Rasula, "Placing *Pieces*," *Sagetrieb* 1 (1982): 167.

4. THE POETICS OF RECOGNITION

1. Creeley, *Was That a Real Poem and Other Essays*, 15.

2. My reading of this poem depends on the information gathered about it by George Butterick in his *Guide*, 99–108.

3. In *Poet's Prose*, I present an argument for the importance of paratactic syntax in the pursuit of truth by American prose poetry.

4. See Reznikoff's poem, "The English in Virginia, April 1607," *Poems 1918–1936*, vol. 1 of *The Complete Poems of Charles Reznikoff*, ed. Seamus Cooney (Santa Barbara, Calif.: Black Sparrow Press, 1976), 122–3. See Butterick's *Guide*, 79–80, 103, for citations of Olson's high opinion of Smith as a writer.

5. See Pound's *Gaudier-Brzeska* (1916; rpt. New York: New Directions, 1970), 46, for his oft-repeated claim that the artist could read Chinese ideograms by sheer visual acuity.

6. One could begin to map out this pervasive "circuit" of nature, word, and experience by stringing together three critical studies: Sacvan Bercovitch's *Puritan Origins of the American Self* (New Haven: Yale Univ. Press, 1975), which chronicles the ways early American writers adapted biblical typology to their own attempts at self-definition through nature and contemporary history; John Irwin's *American Hieroglyphics* (Baltimore: Johns Hopkins Univ. Press, 1980), which analyzes the fascination of American Renaissance writers with the hieroglyph as a model of literary activity; and Laszlo Géfin's *Ideogram*, which builds from a reading of the Ideogrammic Method in Pound's writing to a preliminary consideration of this method in Williams, the objectivists, the projectivists, Ginsberg, and Snyder.

7. Ernest Fenollosa, *The Chinese Written Character as a Medium for Poetry,* ed. Ezra Pound (1920; rpt. San Francisco: City Lights Books, 1963), 40–41.
8. It is interesting to note that Enyalion proves his virility through offering himself to the gaze of women rather than through composing a woman by gazing at her. Although this sort of self-presentation makes no room for the display of a woman's difference, it does slightly open up gender categories by recognizing a necessary vulnerability in the construction of masculine identity.

5.   CIRCLES AND BOUNDARIES

1. The tropes of circles, circumference, and even containment are primary critical tools in Albert Gelpi's *Tenth Muse,* particularly in the chapters on Edward Taylor, Emerson, Whitman, and Dickinson. Gelpi uses these tropes to explore psychological issues in the poetry, especially the relation between inner and outer worlds.
2. In *American Visionary Poetry* (Baton Rouge: Louisiana State Univ. Press, 1982), Hyatt H. Waggoner discusses the importance of the eye to visionary poetry in a whole range of American poets.
3. "Pages from a Notebook," 1953; rpt. Donald Allen, ed., *The New American Poetry* (New York: Grove Press, 1960), 407. Duncan's statement echoes Williams's introduction to *The Wedge* (1944), in which he claims that "the arts generally are not, nor is this writing a diversion from [the war] for relief, a turning away. It *is* the war or part of it, merely a different sector of the field" (Williams, *Selected Essays* [1954; rpt. New York: New Directions, 1969], 255). In Book Three of *Paterson,* "The Library," Williams depicts a parallel conflagration of culture to the one Emerson identifies ([New York: New Directions, 1963], 137–49). Following Williams, Olson also finds a thrill in creative destruction in his poem "La Torre": "The end of something has a satisfaction. / When the structures go, light / comes through" (*CP,* 189).
4. For an important discussion of whim and abandonment in Emerson, see Cavell, *Senses,* 136–8. In his essay on Thoreau, Emerson specifically faults Thoreau for his relentless containment: "I cannot help counting it a fault in him that he had no ambition. Wanting this, instead of engineering for all America, he was the captain of a huckleberry party. Pounding beans is good to the end of pounding empires one of these days; but if, at the end of years, it is still only beans!" (*RWE,* 427).
5. Byrd, "The Question of Wisdom as Such," in Bertholf and Reid, eds., *Robert Duncan,* 38–9.
6. Robert Duncan, "Notes toward the Structure of Rime," *Maps* 6 (1974): 44.
7. Jonathan Bishop, *Emerson on the Soul* (Cambridge, Mass.: Harvard Univ. Press, 1964), 2.
8. For an earlier discussion of not-understanding in poetry, see my *Poet's Prose,* 2d ed., 108–12, 116–17.
9. Bruns, "What Is Tradition?" 8.

10. For a discussion of hermeneutics as an inheritance from Hermes, see Richard E. Palmer, *Hermeneutics* (Evanston, Ill.: Northwestern Univ. Press, 1969), 12–15. H.D. invokes Hermes in many of the same ways that Duncan does, in her *Trilogy,* particularly during the first book, *The Walls Do Not Fall.* For a summary discussion of the importance of Hermes in that text, see Albert Gelpi, *A Coherent Splendor: The American Poetic Renaissance, 1910–1950* (Cambridge: Cambridge Univ. Press, 1987), 290–2.

11. A vivid depiction of the cultish world of San Francisco that Olson fears can be found in the films of Duncan's associate Kenneth Anger, such as *Scorpio Rising* and *Inauguration of the Pleasure Dome.* In "Marginality in the Margins: Robert Duncan's Textual Politics" (*Contemporary Literature* 33 [1992]: 275–301), Michael Davidson argues that for Duncan the issue of boundaries and their transgression always bears the import of his sexual struggles as "The Homosexual in Society" (to quote the title of his groundbreaking essay of 1944).

12. For a more balanced, careful assessment of the poetic community in San Francisco, see Michael Davidson, *The San Francisco Renaissance.*

13. The invocation of Thomas the Rimer is particularly rich in associations. The actual man, Thomas of Erceldoune, was a thirteenth-century poet said to have the power of prophecy, as proven by his foretelling the death of the king of Scotland in a famous battle. Author of a romance and ballads, Thomas himself became a figure in ballads, in the most familiar of which he becomes the consort of the Queen of the Elves, spends seven years with her in Elfland, and receives "the tongue that never can lee [lie]" (*Norton Anthology of English Literature,* 4th ed., 1: 399). In addition to his prophetic sight and his truth-telling abilities, Thomas the Rimer serves Duncan by recalling the "Structure of Rime" series of poems that begins in the same book, *The Opening of the Field,* in which this poem is found. Also, Thomas's adventures underground with the Queen of the Elves resonate not only with other passages within this particular poem – for instance, "('Good People' we called them – another folk / that work underground)" (*OF,* 91) – but also with other poems in the book, such as the opening poem, "Often I Am Permitted to Return to a Meadow," which invokes a "First Beloved" who initiates the poet into poetry: "She it is Queen Under The Hill / whose hosts are a disturbance of words within words / that is a field folded" (*OF,* 7).

14. For an in-depth portrait of Duncan's rejection of middle–class values, see Ekbert Faas, *Young Robert Duncan: Portrait of the Poet as Homosexual in Society* (Santa Barbara, Calif.: Black Sparrow Press, 1983), especially the chapters "Childhood," "Adolescence," and "Berkeley Interlude."

15. Donald Pease, *Visionary Compacts: American Renaissance Writings in Cultural Context* (Madison: Univ. of Wisconsin Press, 1987), 231.

16. I have discussed the sentence's claim to completeness in *Poet's Prose,* 2d ed., 32–41. For a brief consideration of Duncan's prose poetry, see ibid., 95–100.

17. F. O. Matthiessen, *American Renaissance: Art and Expression in the Age of Emerson and Whitman* (New York: Oxford Univ. Press, 1941), 55–6. In-

terestingly, in his acknowledgments to the volume, Mathiessen mentions, among friends "who have been engaged in the same field," Charles Olson: "Olson's generosity in letting me make use of what he has tracked down in his investigation of Melville's reading, particularly Melville's markings in his volumes of Hawthorne, alone made possible my study of their inter-relation" (xviii). Olson's tracking down, discovering, and analyzing of the volumes in Melville's library was his first attempt at a "saturation job," which resulted both in a signal contribution to Melville scholarship and in *Call Me Ishmael* (1947), Olson's first major prose grounding for his poetry.

18. "Poetry and Imagination," vol. 8 of *Works of Ralph Waldo Emerson,* ed. Edward Waldo Emerson (Boston: Houghton Mifflin, 1904), 50.

19. "To Lydia Jackson, Concord, February 1, 1835," *Letters of Ralph Waldo Emerson,* ed. Ralph L. Rusk (New York: Columbia Univ. Press, 1939), 1: 435.

20. Duncan repeats Emerson's prescription, updating the terms slightly, in the following statement: "As the story told of stars and subatomic particles and the story told of living organisms continue to reorient our possible knowl-edge of what is, the poetic imagination faces the challenge of finding a structure that will be the complex story of all the stories felt to be true, a myth in which something like the variety of man's experience of what is real may be contained" (*FC,* 6). Notice how in this passage, too, Duncan sub-stitutes "myth" for Emerson's master term "nature."

21. In volume 3 of *The Maximus Poems,* love and self-identity come together in the moving, sacrificial poetry of Olson's last days.

22. Compare Duncan's relationship to forgetfulness and remembrance to that of Heidegger, as explained by Gerald Bruns: " 'Wherever concealment of beings as a whole is conceded only as a limit that occasionally announces itself, concealing as a fundamental occurrence has sunk into forgetfulness' (Wm 90/134). It is part of the work of the work of art, that is, its truth, not to allow this forgetfulness of concealment, of the truth of un-truth, to occur. This is because concealment belongs to the truth of the work as to truth itself." *Heidegger's Estrangements,* 33–4.

23. Robert Duncan, "Preface to a Reading of Passages 1–22," *Maps* 6 (1974): 53.

24. Michael Davidson, "A Book of First Things: *The Opening of the Field,*" in Bertholf and Reid, eds., *Robert Duncan,* 57. Davidson discusses the image of the field on pp. 57–61.

25. *Herakleitos and Diogenes,* trans. Guy Davenport (Bolinas, Calif.: Grey Fox Press, 1979), 29.

6. CONCLUSION

1. *Whitman: Selected by Robert Creeley* (Harmondsworth, Eng.: Penguin, 1973), 7.

2. *The Collected Poems of William Carlos Williams: Vol. II, 1939–1962* (New York: New Directions, 1988), 245.

3. *Later* (New York: New Directions, 1979), 4–5.

4. *The Collected Poems of Robert Creeley: 1945–1975* (Berkeley: Univ. of California Press, 1982), 395–6 (ellipsis Creeley's).

5. And for Duncan, the mothers (such as H.D., Gertrude Stein, and Edith Sitwell) unsettle the whole patriarchal tradition, authorizing every sort of affiliation.

6. Jack R. Cohn and Thomas J. O'Donnell, "An Interview with Robert Duncan," *Contemporary Literature* 21 (1980): 524.

7. Duncan's "Poem Beginning with a Line by Pindar" meditates at length upon so many of the issues associated with tradition for American poets. In the fourth section, Duncan uses these same images of a psychic "clearing held against indians" (*OF*, 68). He then goes on to affirm the relationship between history and tradition, on the one hand, and love, death, and destruction, on the other, imaging the double giving and withholding in a dance of children "clockwise and counter-clockwise turning" (*OF*, 69).

8. "Notes on Grossinger's *Solar Journal: Oecological Sections*" (Los Angeles: Black Sparrow Press, 1970), n.p.

9. For a discussion of American literature as provincial in relation to English, see Geoffrey Thurley, *The American Moment: American Poetry in the Mid-Century* (New York: St. Martin's Press, 1977), especially the first chapter.

10. *Collected Poems, II*, 284.

INDEX

165

CAMBRIDGE STUDIES IN AMERICAN LITERATURE AND CULTURE

Continued from the front of the book

169

17. ANN KIBBEY, *The Interpretation of Material Shapes in Puritanism: A Study of Rhetoric, Prejudice, and Violence*

16. SACVAN BERCOVITCH and MYRA JEHLEN, (eds.), *Ideology and Classic American Literature*

15. LAWRENCE BUELL, *New England Literary Culture: From Revolution Through Renaissance*

14. PAUL GILES, *Hart Crane: The Contexts of "The Bridge"*

13. ALBERT GELPI (ed.), *Wallace Stevens: The Poetics of Modernism*

12. ALBERT J. VON FRANK, *The Sacred Game: Provincialism and Frontier Consciousness in American Literature, 1630–1860*

11. DAVID WYATT, *The Fall into Eden: Landscape and Imagination in California*

10. ELIZABETH MCKINSEY, *Niagara Falls: Icon of the American Sublime*

9. BARTON LEVI ST. ARMAND, *Emily Dickinson and Her Culture: The Soul's Society*

8. MITCHELL BREITWIESER, *Cotton Mather and Benjamin Franklin: The Price of Representative Personality*

7. PETER CONN, *The Divided Mind: Ideology and Imagination in America, 1898–1917*

6. MARJORIE PERLOFF, *The Dance of the Intellect: Studies in the Poetry of the Pound Tradition*

The following books in the series are out of print

5. STEPHEN FREDMAN, *Poet's Prose: The Crisis in American Verse*, first edition

4. PATRICIA CALDWELL, *The Puritan Conversion Narrative: The Beginnings of American Expression*

3. JOHN P. MCWILLIAMS, JR., *Hawthorne, Melville, and the American Character: A Looking-Glass Business*

2. CHARLES ALTIERI, *Self and Sensibility in Contemporary American Poetry*

1. ROBERT ZALLER, *The Cliffs of Solitude: A Reading of Robinson Jeffers*